An estimated 5 in 10,000 children : tism. Now there is a reliable, compr ents—a complete sourcebook of a encouraging testimony that *you are not alone in facing the complex challenges of autism.*

A PARENT'S GUIDE TO AUTISM
discusses in detail such questions as:

Are all people with autism alike?

If my child scores low on an I.Q. test, is he autistic?

Is autism caused by the parents and could we have done anything to prevent it?

Can allergies cause autistic behavior?

What's the difference between autism and pervasive developmental disabilities (PDD)?

If autism is a birth defect, why does it take years for the effects to show up?

How does the "education for all" law affect my child's schooling?

. . . and much, much more.

———————————————

"Thoughtful articulate, realistic, yet hopeful, *A PARENT'S GUIDE TO AUTISM* is neither too simple nor too complicated. It presents accurate, sophisticated, and important information about autism in a way that all people can understand. I assure readers that they will learn a great deal about autism, human resilience, and heroism in the pages that follow."
—*Gary B. Mesibov, Ph.D.*,
University of North Carolina at Chapel Hill

A PARENT'S
GUIDE TO
AUTISM

Charles A. Hart

POCKET BOOKS

New York   London   Toronto   Sydney   Tokyo   Singapore

The author of this book is not a physician and reminds you that he does not intend the ideas, procedures, and suggestions in this book to substitute for the medical advice of a trained health professional. All matters regarding your child's health require medical supervision. Consult your child's physician before adopting the suggestions in this book, as well as about any condition that may require diagnosis or medical attention. The author and publisher disclaim any liability arising directly or indirectly from the use of the book.

An *Original* Publication of POCKET BOOKS

POCKET BOOKS, a division of Simon & Schuster Inc.
1230 Avenue of the Americas, New York, NY 10020

Hart, Charles, 1940–
    A parent's guide to autism / by Charles A. Hart.
        p.   cm.
    Includes bibliographical references.
    ISBN: 0-671-75099-2
    1. Autism in children—Miscellanea. I. Title.
RJ506.A9H28   1993
618.9289'82—dc20   93-9438
                                           CIP

First Pocket Books trade paperback printing June 1993

10 9 8 7 6 5 4

POCKET and colophon are registered trademarks of Simon & Schuster Inc.

Cover design by Tom McKeveny

Printed in the U.S.A.

Contents

Dedicated to Albert Reichert, M.D.,
the doctor who inspired us to learn
all we could about autism
and share it with other families.

Introduction

To understand autism, or any other human condition, you must observe the individuals, not just the stereotypes. Our most talented teachers agree when they say, "To reach a child with autism, you must first learn to see the world through the student's eyes."

Hopefully, this book will encourage you to read more about autism, because the future should bring even better news than we can share today. Research has made steady progress, but no one can answer all of your questions today, or predict your particular child's future.

We all want a cure for our child, and we want that cure as soon as possible. It's natural to grow impatient with the pace of progress, but medical research proceeds at a rate we can't control. Even the best treatments and therapies have limitations. Some work better with certain types of people than they do with others, and some simply don't live up to their promoters' claims. No one has discovered a remedy for every symptom of autism. There are simply too many problems to solve with one cure-all.

Parents and researchers are always looking for better treatments, and, while there's no perfect solution, progress is very encouraging. After all, this disability wasn't even known a lifetime ago. The year 1993 marks the fiftieth anniversary of Dr. Leo Kanner's decision to coin the term *autism*. He chose that word because he thought it described his patients' tendency to act "automated," or self-contained.

Fifty years ago, children weren't given the diagnosis of autism, no one recognized this disorder, and families had no place to turn for information. Those children were simply born too soon. Many of them are still alive today, including my brother.

In the 1920s, he was a quiet little boy who couldn't phrase sentences of his own but merely echoed fragments of other peoples' speech. Since there was no "education for all" law, he never went to school. Nor did he have language therapy, because no one had developed the techniques that would one day teach children like him to speak.

No one understood his learning problems, or recognized his potential, so they called him retarded. He grew up to become what people expected him to be: a childlike adult who needs constant supervision.

A generation later, my son was born. When he developed learning problems like his uncle's, my wife and I began looking for help, just as my parents had fifty years earlier. The progress we saw inspired us. The disability no longer seemed hopeless!

We found professionals who had worked with children like our son. They showed us patterns in his language and behavior that we had overlooked. We had seen problems, odd examples of play and language, but, like so many parents, we were too close to our child to see the "big picture." Along the way, we learned that neither my son nor my brother are alone with their challenge, for there may be three hundred thousand people with similar problems just in the United States.

We never found the cure for our son, but we found doctors, teachers, occupational therapists, and communication therapists. They helped us understand the connections between our son's noticeable behaviors and his invisible biological problems. Together, we prepared him for a life he enjoys, independent enough to work and balance a checkbook and social enough to bore his co-workers with "knock-knock" jokes.

Ted isn't perfect; he's human. Twenty years ago we

wanted a miracle that would make our son's life better than his uncle's had been. The miracle didn't come in a flash of light, or a quick response to treatment, so we didn't notice, until looking through our family album. Then we saw the miracle. School pictures, including graduation and the senior prom, showed how rich our son's life had become. How rich it could have been for my brother, if he'd been born in 1970, instead of 1920!

If your child is even younger than mine, he or she will be even luckier. Each year seems to bring better services and better understanding of autism. We don't have all of the answers yet. We still wonder why some therapies help certain people, but not others. However, we know more than ever before. Most important, we know better than to call a person "hopeless" or place an imaginary ceiling on a person's abilities, just because she has problems with expression.

To understand autism, or any other human condition, you must observe individuals, not just stereotypes. Today, our most talented teachers say, "To reach a child with autism, you must first learn to see the world through the student's eyes." Add to that: "And hear the world through his ears, feel it through his body, and experience it through his sense of time."

Ask yourself, "What would I do if I couldn't express myself through words?" or "How could I learn if the teacher's sounds didn't seem to match the gestures?" Your questions, like the answers, must be individual, for people with autism don't all have the same learning problems.

This book encourages you to ask many questions. Readers who ask the right questions will make better choices for their daughters or sons with autism. If we do our job well, our children will reward us by reaching their own potential, not by becoming a copy of someone else.

1

What Is Autism?

The words *autism* and *autistic* have often been misused in the press and on the street. The misinformation is more frightening than the reality. Understanding this disability is the first step on a pathway of hope and progress.

Autism is the term used to describe a variety of neurological problems that affect thought, perception, and attention. This disability can block, delay, or distort signals from the eyes, the ears, and other sensory organs. This usually weakens a person's ability to interact with other people, either through social activity or using communication skills such as speech. It may also limit abilities such as imagination and reasoning.

In some cases, infants can show signs of this disability. A baby may stare into space instead of making eye contact. She may ignore voices, refuse to cuddle, or even resist touching. Most often, autism goes undetected in children until they are two and a half or three years old, the age when a child should show sudden progress in language and imaginative play.

The signs of autism first appear as developmental delay. The child is slower than most to reach milestones of babbling or meaningful speech, making social gestures such as smiling or touching another person. Authorities classify autism as a "developmental disability" because it interferes with the rate or sequence of childhood development.

5

As with other developmental disabilities, such as mental retardation and cerebral palsy, the condition usually lasts a lifetime, but that doesn't mean the person can't learn. Approaches to education are discussed in Chapter 13.

The human brain is the most complicated organ on this planet. It goes through many stages of organization and growth from the early months in our mother's womb, through infancy, childhood, and on into adult life. Although no two human beings develop identically, most of us learn to walk, talk, and reason following a fairly predictable timetable.

Parents should look at developmental charts to check whether their child sits up, turns over, and babbles at the typical age. Some youngsters take longer than others to pass through certain stages. They may catch up, or master other skills on time. However, a few newborns appear slow from birth. If you think your child has missed a developmental stage, bring it to his doctor's or teacher's attention.

Parents shouldn't feel guilty if they don't recognize their child's autism before her second or third birthday. We don't expect our children to have this disability and few of us know what to look for. It's hard, even for professionals, to recognize the signs of autism in an infant. Most of these children seem pretty typical until the toddler years, when they show difficulty with language, play, and social interaction.

In unusual cases, a child's difficulties may go unrecognized until the teen years, when the parents realize their daughter or son has problems that fit the pattern of autism. Many people who should have this diagnosis are mistakenly called brain damaged or mentally ill, or given some other label. Since no one really knows how often autism goes unrecognized or misdiagnosed, it's hard to find agreement in the statistics. Estimates of the number of people with autism range from 4 to 5 out of every 10,000 to 15 to 20 per 10,000.

The difficulty of diagnosis will be discussed in Chapter 5. Some day we may learn to diagnose autism through brain scans and/or chemical measurements. However, at this time we rely on certain behaviors and test scores to recognize autism.

What are the symptoms?

Judging accurately how often autism occurs is doubly difficult because, though medical research has explored many possible testing methods, no biological screening—whether tests of body fluids, allergy screening, or brain scans—gives a reliable prediction or measurement of autism.

Throughout the years, various authorities have offered different checklists of behaviors that indicate autism. Chapter 2 describes behaviors associated with autism in more detail. Opinions still vary about the specific behaviors tied to autism and their importance, or the score a person has to rate on an autism measurement scale in order for the diagnosis to be made. However, most professionals trained in this field agree on these important symptoms:

Language delay and/or deficits: Most people with autism show difficulties in the use and understanding of language, but they don't all have the same developmental pattern, or the same outcome. Approximately 20 percent don't speak, but will learn sign language or typing. Others may have to learn primitive communication skills, such as gesturing or pointing at pictures to indicate objects of need or desire.

A few children begin speaking like typical children until the age of eighteen to twenty months, but then suddenly lose the ability.

Many who can speak merely repeat other peoples' words instead of creating their own sentences. Some show confusion about pronouns. For example, they don't use *I* and *you* correctly or understand when other speakers shift from being me to being *you*.

Social problems and difficulty with relationships: In extreme cases very young children may appear antisocial, resist cuddling, or avoid the touch of others. Some people with autism seem to show no interest in other people. They may avoid affection or don't appear to love their own families. However, they may actually have the same emotions as other people. Perhaps they avoid affection or eye contact because they respond differently to common sensations like a soft touch on the arm or the sight of Mom's smile. Occupational therapists can help parents understand how a child's sensory problems affect social behavior.

Unusual reactions to sound, sight, taste, touch, or smell: Most of us have fairly typical reactions to the five senses, but people with autism often show unusual responses. Some appear especially sensitive (hypersensitive) or under sensitive (hyposensitive) to common sensations. A person hypersensitive to sound may find household noises painfully loud, even frightening. Hyposensitivity to noise makes it hard to notice or recognize common sounds.

An individual with autism may have unusual responses to any, or even all, of the five basic senses. It is possible to have hypersensitivity to some and hyposensitivity to others. No particular combination of sensory problems is typical of autism. However, unusual responses to sensations indicate a neurological problem, possibly autism.

Uneven developmental abilities, scattered strengths and weaknesses: Standard I.Q. tests like Stanford-Binet and Wechsler and most other measurements of intelligence prove unreliable for people with autism. This is because those tests are structured to measure the intelligence of a person who has typical vision, hearing, and forms of experience. We know children with autism simply don't get the same array of signals from their environment. They may have extraordinary perception in areas the test won't acknowledge, while they probably have deficits in other areas that lower their test scores.

Psychologists who test children with autism expect to see signs of uneven development because these children have some skills that are normal, or even superior, for their age, and others that show significant delay.

Some tests are designed to measure very specific abilities, such as gross motor or fine motor coordination. Tests of language ability show two measurements, one for understanding and one for application. Parents usually dread their child's first developmental examination. They don't know what to expect and fear that the "experts" will hang a label like retarded or hopeless on their child.

A four-year-old we'll call Richard illustrates how widely a child's intelligence can vary: he speaks—when he wants to, but his language is usually nonsense. He seems to hear everything, but rarely follows instructions. He ignores other children, preferring to play alone. The concepts of sharing or turn-taking haven't occurred to him. He's already a social dropout, taking the toys that interest him off into a corner, where he will sit for long periods of time, stacking blocks or lining plastic figures in a row.

He walks a little awkwardly and his mother noted he didn't sit up or stand quite as soon as she expected from reading charts on early development. He still can't alternate feet going downstairs, but always begins with the left and places his right foot on the same step before moving the left one on to the next level.

Richard perks up when he recognizes pictures of Sesame Street characters. He easily recognizes letters and numbers when the testor questions him, but he looks blank and remains silent when the examiner asks questions about "more" or "less."

His test results—ranging from a "severely low" score of 20 in social skills and speech to a "superior intelligence" of 120 in academic ability—baffle Richard's mother. His language understanding and gross motor skills scores are in the near-normal range of 80. And his fine motor skills seem perfectly typical for his age.

When a child with autism is tested in several skills areas, each score may suggest a different intelligence quotient (I.Q.). But none of these scores, nor even a statistical average of all the scores, will predict the child's potential. Performance of most tasks requires skill in more than one testing area. To succeed in most tasks at school or at work, you need to recognize instructions (process language input), coordinate your body movements (have fine and gross motor coordination), and articulate your responses (use both expressive language and social skills).

I.Q. scores won't tell you what your child can do so much as they'll identify areas of strength and weakness. You'll maximize success when you discover how to stimulate your child's talents and find ways to work around or compensate for his or her weaknesses.

Tests such as CARS (Childhood Autism Rating Scale), developed by Dr. Eric Schopler at the University of North Carolina, should be used in cases of autism. CARS will help confirm the diagnosis of autism and provide more reliable information about a child's ability level and learning style.

Recent research suggests that people with autism often have higher intelligence than we have recognized. However, the communication disorder makes it hard for individuals with autism to interact with their parents and teachers to demonstrate this. Chapter 11 raises more questions about intelligence, and its relation to communication abilities

How can you tell if a person has autism?

The signs of language delay, social problems, sensory disturbance, and uneven skill development may all point toward the diagnosis of autism. However, other neurological problems such as stroke or traumatic head injury could cause similar symptoms. We call autism a developmental disability because the symptoms show up in the process of development, not as specific reactions to injury or illness.

You must look at a person's developmental history to recognize a pattern that indicates autism. Do medical records show health problems or accidents that might have caused brain damage after birth? At what age did the child begin to appear unusual? What signs concerned the parents first? Speech delay? Lack of interest in other people? Failure to respond to sound or other sensations? Overreaction to touch?

The parents, or others who know the person's history, should list everything unusual about the childhood. When did he or she reach milestones such as first steps or first words? When did unusual behaviors like hand-flapping or walking on her toes begin? How long did they last? What has the family tried to help the child and how did he or she react? What seems to "reach" this individual, make him pay attention, please him and motivate him?

A doctor or psychologist trained to diagnose autism needs to observe the individual. As parent, you will be interviewed or asked to fill out questionnaires to sketch in the developmental history. Finally, an examination such as an intelligence test designed for people with language difficulties may complete the diagnosis.

Most family doctors and psychologists have so little experience with this disability that they refer the family to specialists to make the official diagnosis.

Are there different types of autism?

Absolutely! Individuals with autism vary in their intelligence, their response to sensation, and their communication skill. The differences between people with autism are so great that professionals often argue about the use of the term *autism*. For example, we know that some people with autism can drive a car, earn a college degree, and publish their autobiography, while still dealing with social limitations and personal eccentricities.

At the other extreme, some people with autism never learn to express themselves or practice acceptable social behaviors. They may have problems of aggression, violence, even self-abuse. In the past, some people were considered "hopeless," but we're getting better at teaching people with severe disabilities. Education and social tolerance are powerful factors in determining a child's chances in the future.

In medical terms autism is generally called a syndrome, rather than a specific condition. *Syndrome* implies more than one form with more than one cause or influence. High blood pressure, for instance, is a syndrome affected by several factors such as diet, stress, heredity, and possibly other influences.

Is there a difference between autism and mental retardation?

This question raises another, What is mental retardation? *Mental retardation* is a term drawn from the French word, *retardé*, which simply means "late," or "delayed." Psychologists and educators use this term to describe a learner whose skill lags at least 20 percent behind the average person. The more delayed the learning, the more serious the retardation appears.

We measure retardation in terms of the rate of learning, or the person's abilities as compared with a typical person of the same age. It has no medical meaning. However, many different medical problems could have been the cause of the learning delay that became labeled as retardation. For example, genetic disorders like Down syndrome. Head injury, poor nutrition, and lack of oxygen to the brain can all affect a person's ability to learn and perform on tests of intelligence. But *mental retardation* is not a medical condition, it is a broad term for learning disabilities resulting from many different medical problems.

Since most people with autism have trouble in one or more developmental areas (language, reasoning, planning, etc.), they generally appear retarded when given standard intelligence tests. Most tests simply can't distinguish between a generally slow learner and one whose delay is due to other, more selective developmental problems.

From an educator's point of view, there's an important difference between autism and the other serious learning disorders. Autism usually affects very specific neurological pathways, leaving others unharmed or even strengthened. The learner with autism often has unusual strengths; an extraordinary sense of direction, self-taught reading, or an ability to memorize an astonishing series of numbers. Teachers have the challenge of finding the individual student's best pathways to learning.

A casual observer might not see a difference between students with autism and those with general retardation. The students may appear similar, sharing problems with grooming, personal hygiene and other self-help skills. They might even score in the same range on tests of motor development and speech. But observant teachers find that children with autism have hidden skills. When trained in their areas of strength, these students may learn more than the children with other developmental problems.

What is a developmental disability?

The phrase *developmental disability* came into use as a legal term in the 1970s. For the purpose of social policy planning and federal funding, social and political organizations wanted to name an entire group of conditions that challenged the individual's ability to learn and function independently. Federally and state-funded programs addressing these disabilities then became the first agencies to use the term *developmental disabilities*.

Many agencies that used to speak of *mental retardation* changed over to use the newer term. However, the legal definition of *developmental disability* includes autism, cerebral palsy, and epilepsy, as well as mental retardation. The intent is to describe any disabling condition that affects the intellectual, functional, and/or academic development of an individual. A developmental disability must occur before the age of twenty-one to meet the federal definition. This can qualify a person for services, such as special education, Supplemental Security Income, and Medicaid.

Many government regulations and insurance policies

stress a difference between services for people with developmental disabilities and those with mental health conditions. For example, policies often exclude mental health services, but cover educational or habilitative services. Accordingly, parents have to make sure the insurance company doesn't misclassify autism as mental illness. Such a mistaken classification could disqualify a child for services such as occupational therapy or communication therapy.

Are there different terms for this disability?

More often than not, the first professionals to notice the child's unusual development will diagnose "pervasive development delay (PDD)," or "autistic-like" behaviors. Many families complain that each teacher or doctor describes their child in different terms.

While some forms of autism can best be described by special terms like Rett syndrome or fragile X (described in Chapter 4), many of the labels used during diagnosis mean very little. Calling a child "atypical" or "retarded with autistic characteristics" is not making a precise diagnosis. But many professionals lack the experience and confidence to write the word *autism* on a child's medical chart or school record.

Why does *autism* mean so many different things to so many different people?

People get their impression of autism through exposure, either to individuals with the disability or to published information or television shows, and even through mere gossip. It's no wonder that so many people have such confused or misinformed opinions about what autism is and what people with autism are like.

Part of the confusion surrounding the word grows out of the history of its use. The term came into our medical terminology as recently as 1943 when Dr. Leo Kanner chose the Greek root-word, *auto*, to describe this condition that seemed to keep people from interacting with others, making them appear self-absorbed and separate.

Since 1943 the word *autism* has had an unfortunate history. For many years people thought it meant an emotional disorder, a child's decision to reject first his parents, then the world. Twenty years ago many medical dictionaries defined autism as "a morbid self-absorption to the exclusion of external stimuli."

Unfortunately, this primitive misunderstanding of the neurological disorder was widely spread through books like *The Empty Fortress*. The fantasy that people with autism have special secrets or have chosen to shut out the world still shows up in popular literature and on some television shows. The word has taken on a symbolic and usually false meaning for the purposes of show business or common conversation that has nothing to do with today's wider understanding from serious research in medicine and psychology.

Where can I find out more?

Since 1943, professionals have offered many theories to explain autism and suggest treatments. Most of the early writings now appear useless, except as history of early theories.

Always look at the newest professional publications on this subject. The *Journal of Autism and Developmental Disorders* gives the most reliable coverage of new research on autism. The information printed there has been reviewed by an editorial board that includes some of the world's leading authorities in medicine, education, psychology, and other fields that serve people with autism.

Most states and many large communities have a chapter of the Autism Society of America. This organization and its many local branches offer free information to parents and the general public. Some maintain lending libraries and/or book stores. If your phone book doesn't have a listing under

"Autism Society of [your town or state]," see Chapter 16 for a listing of national organizations, including the Autism Society of America. Call or write to find out about their chapter nearest your home.

A number of families have published personal stories about their experiences with autism. The next chapter will review several in detail. Chapter 16 has an even longer list of books written by individuals with autism and their parents. Though the unique experiences of a particular family won't necessarily prove helpful to others whose child has different challenges and experiences, they may offer insight and support.

Be cautious about believing every magazine or newspaper article that announces a "cure" for autism. Commercial publishers and broadcasters don't have the same standards of scientific proof and analysis that you will find in professional publications.

REVIEW

Autism is a neurological disorder that affects an individual's ability to process information from the senses and different areas of the brain. The basis for this neurological problem probably begins before birth but often can't be recognized until several years later when the child shows problems developing skills common to others of the same age. Since the rate and pattern of development is the primary concern with autism, we call it a "developmental disability," as opposed to any form of mental illness.

The primary challenges for people with autism include language development and other forms of human interaction, including the subtle gestures of facial expression, tone of voice, and body language—features of what we call the total communication. For this reason we often call autism a "communication disorder" and look to communication therapy as an important aid for the individual.

2

What Are People with Autism Like?

People with autism don't use gestures such as a friendly look, lilting voice, and gentle touch to express affection. Their neurological differences keep them from mastering the "universal language of love," but that doesn't mean they don't love. They just can't express their feelings in a way that we always recognize.

"Mysterious" and "baffling": We often hear those words from people who don't understand autism. Our first impressions of a person with autism are confusing. Though the individual probably looks as normal as you or me, her behavior is not. In fact, there are no external physical signs—hearing aids, wheel chairs, or white canes—to show that the person has this disability.

People with autism don't look different from others; that is, until we look at their facial expressions, body language, and gestures. Then we begin to notice the differences. They show unusual reactions to common situations, or they may show no reaction at all.

They may laugh at the "wrong" time in a movie, during a scene others find sad or frightening. Perhaps they cry or show fear when we don't expect it—panic at the sight of a clown or show distress during a hymn at church. Some of them appear to ignore sounds, sights, and events that involve them. These are people who don't seem to share our world of sensations and meanings. Their reasons for behaving and feeling are hidden by a veil of privacy that some writers have called a wall or a shell.

People with autism can't explain their behavior to us. First of all, most of them have difficulty with language. Furthermore, they don't realize that their experience of the world is different from the average person's. Simply put, we confuse them as much as they baffle us.

Chapter 11 will explore some of the reasons behind their behavior, but first we will look at behavior as symptoms, clues that the person has an unusual neurological system. We can't see inside the person's mind, so we must watch what we can see, the obvious external behaviors that suggest thought patterns different from the average person's.

What are children with autism like?

Since autism is a developmental disability, we can't say that a certain behavior at any particular point in time is proof of autism. Far from it. Each of us goes through a wide variety of moods, periods of activity and rest, even days when we feel we are "not ourselves." The accidental and spontaneous events in our lives may cause unpredictable feelings or behaviors in everyone. So we don't call a person autistic on the basis of a single impression.

Rather than a still picture, we need to look at a moving picture, a documentary, the story of the child's development as he or she goes through the changes from infant to toddler and on. We may recognize autism in a child by some of these clues:

> A) Unusual responses to environment such as overreaction or lack of reaction to sight, sound, or touch
> B) Problems with spoken language

C) Problems making friends and understanding others
D) Odd play
E) Uneven development

A) *Unusual responses to environment,* such as overreacting or underreacting to sight, sound, or touch: Some children with autism begin life as fussy babies who cry more than the average. These infants may sleep fitfully and scream at contact with their parents.

You can't diagnose autism merely by an infant's behavior, since many babies go through fussy stages. However, when a toddler or older child still shrieks at certain sounds, fears flashes of light, or tries to avoid a mother's touch, it means the youngster probably hears, or sees, or feels, too intensely—all signs of a highly arousable, unstable nervous system. Some of these children are also physically overactive. But none of these signs by themselves prove autism. Other medical problems could explain these conditions. Perhaps the child will just outgrow them.

On the other hand, babies who seem unusually calm and easy to care for may show symptoms of autism during the toddler stage. What the parents mistook for a "good nature" in infancy might be the first indication that this youngster isn't disturbed by sights and sounds—because he hadn't noticed them. The child who is hyposensitive (undersensitive) won't wake up or cry as often as the hypersensitive (oversensitive child). But neither will he pick up as much information from his environment. He may have a deficit of attention, making it hard to tune in to signals from his environment.

Many children with autism seem pretty typical until the age of two or three. Some even appear gifted or unusually intelligent. They may stare at things that interest them and appear to study them at an early age. No one can tell if these children have autism until they've had time to show more of their developmental destiny.

B) *Problems with speech:* Typical youngsters begin babbling around six months, speaking first words at a year, and chaining two or three words together by eighteen months. Children with autism, on the other hand, have no common pattern of language development. They vary tremendously; some never speak, some sound like typical youngsters up to the age of eighteen to twenty months, then lose their language and remain speechless during the rest of their lives. Occasionally a child surprises everyone, suddenly beginning to speak at the age of six, after learning to read and write!

More commonly, children with autism show steady but slow progress in language, while still another type speaks on schedule, always sounding as fluent as typical children the same age. Sometimes this fluency conceals problems of understanding and usage, and the language may be repetitive, nonsensical, dysfunctional.

Failure to speak in early childhood isn't necessarily proof of autism. Speech delay can be caused by other factors or be temporary. The real sign of autism is language difficulty over time. Chapter 11 deals with communication disorders in greater length.

C) *Problems making friends and understanding others:* Many children with autism seem to ignore their parents, teachers, and other children. Some never look people in the eye or pay attention to the facial expressions of others.

If they can't read social signals like our smiles and frowns, they may not learn to imitate and so won't respond as we expect, a smile in exchange for a smile. Most don't play games of pretend. Parents and playmates often have trouble understanding these childrens' feelings, so it's hard to play with them since they don't grasp concepts like taking turns and sharing fun. They're left out of group activities, but make no effort to join in. If the child grows older without learning these early social skills, she will have a harder time making friends.

Some children with autism don't understand that each of us has a separate mind and a separate sensory system, thinking different thoughts and registering feelings of pain and pleasure. Instead, they may not understand what hurts or pleases another person and so they may bite, kick, or hit in play, not knowing that it hurts the other person.

They may not understand the boundaries of their own mind and those of others. Some seem to assume everything they know is common knowledge. They expect their parents to "read their mind"; know everything they know without, however, offering their parents enough information to figure that out. They simply don't understand the needs of their listener.

Some don't understand that the function of questions is to get information from another person. Perhaps they can't use questions to get information. They may not know how to solicit or process information from others. Not understanding the give-and-take of communication makes it hard to exchange or share information, no matter how well they can produce speech.

D) Odd play: Children with autism often make strange choices of playthings. They may ignore toys, but play with something unexpected or unusual, preferring scraps of paper, jar lids, or sticks to the bright toys at hand. They may spin, twirl, or stack objects instead of using them in imaginative play.

Even when the child likes a toy, he may use it inappropriately, spinning the wheels on a toy car instead of pushing it along a play road, or carrying puzzle pieces around in his pocket instead of fitting them together to form a whole.

Some children show extreme attachment to objects, carrying them around at all times, insisting on sleeping with their favorites, refusing to put them down in order to use their hands for other activities like eating. Although typical children can go through a phase like this, children with autism earn the championship when it comes to stubbornness or obsession! ◄

Odd forms of play may include hand-flapping, twirling, or rocking. Some children seem to work themselves into a hypnotic trance with sound, motion, or flickering light. Shredding paper, lining up rows of marbles, or repeating a sound over and over again could be a typical childhood activity—a phase—for any toddler. But when a child seems unnaturally preoccupied or spends an unusual amount of time in a particular activity, it may signal a developmental problem, possibly autism.

E) *Uneven development:* Many baby books and doctors' checklists outline the typical time schedule for an infants' growth and learning. Most children follow this developmental calendar on time. However, biological problems sometimes slow a child's physical or mental development in one or more areas, such as physical coordination or language.

A child with autism will probably show delay by the age of thirty months, especially in the areas of speech and social skills. However, that child may have other abilities that measure average or higher, compared to his peers. Such children puzzle us with their combination of skills and weaknesses. Their "cans" and their "can'ts" don't seem to belong to the same person.

If she's doing complicated tasks with her fingers, like drawing, unraveling the curtain cords, and removing handles from the kitchen drawers, but isn't toilet trained at the age of four, she's got a suspiciously uneven developmental pattern.

Perhaps he's memorized the alphabet, knows the name of every street between home and school, but can't play peekaboo as well as his younger brother. Such uneven development is an important symptom of autism. We usually see the first signs in childhood. But the combination of talents and weaknesses generally continues throughout life. A good education will develop the person's strengths, helping them make up for areas of weaknesses.

What are adults with autism like? Do they outgrow their symptoms?

For thirty or forty years autism was considered a childhood disorder. People believed that children outgrew autism and needed to be diagnosed differently in adult life. The terms *infantile autism* and *early childhood schizophrenia* were used only for the developmental years. When the individual grew older, the condition might be called residual autism, mental retardation, or mental illness. Although these beliefs have been discarded by those who follow research in autism, parents need to know that many people still hold them. Unfortunately, the mistaken writings of the past still sit on library shelves and occasionally reappear in the form of magazine articles.

Doctors now understand that autism is a neurological disorder, an unchanging difference in the brain's structure. It is not a chemical cycle or an emotional phase a child can grow out of to emerge whole in later life. Although the brain continues to develop long after birth, the differences found in people with autism don't all disappear.

From a biological or medical point of view, autism is forever. However, the appearance and behavior of a person with autism may very well change, just as maturity and experience make each of us change . . . for better or worse.

Life history affects us all, including people with autism, who are no different in this respect. Opportunities for education, exercise, good health habits, and relationships with others affect all of us by the time we become adults. We should never underestimate the child's potential—to learn or to be happy.

In some ways, adults with autism show many of the characteristics they had in childhood; limited language and social skills, unusual reactions to sensations, odd activities or interests, and the occasional signs of a talent or weakness that seems out of character.

Some childhood behaviors go away; others may be exaggerated in adult life. Early dislikes might become dreaded phobias. The things a child enjoys may become obsessions . . . or be discarded. Predicting the direction of an individual's future is very hard.

As our understanding of autism improves and we make

more progress in education, the future of people with autism looks better and brighter. Already many families have reported that a daughter or son with autism learned skills and achieved goals never thought possible in the past (see Chapter 15, "*What Will the Future Bring?*").

Are all people with autism alike?

Definitely not! In some ways people with autism have less in common with one another than with typical persons. Key differences include:

A) Specific sensory sensitivity
B) Communication abilities
C) Levels of intelligence

A) Specific sensory sensitivity: While some people with autism are extremely sensitive to a particular sensation, such as sound, others may show little or no response. Some will scream in pain at the ring of a telephone, others will appear deaf or indifferent. Some crave spicy foods while others can only stand the mildest flavors.

B) Communication abilities: Some talk freely, while others merely repeat what they have heard, and some will never speak. Most of those who don't speak will be able to use another communication system, such as American Sign Language (developed for the deaf), picture boards (poster boards or sets of pictures students can point to in order to make requests for specific needs such as food, drink, and toilet), or simple gestures like pantomime or acting out needs or desires.

For years we believed that the people who couldn't speak had the lowest level of intelligence. But a new discovery called facilitated communication (see Chapter 12) shows that some individuals are of normal intelligence, in spite of neuromotor problems that make speech impossible.

C) Levels of intelligence: We know that standard I.Q. tests can't estimate the ability of people with language problems, so specialists use other tests to measure the intelligence of people with autism. Some individuals score below 10 on intelligence quotient (profoundly retarded), and others have tested as high as 155 (genius level). Surprisingly, speech ability doesn't seem to be related to overall intelligence.

There are so many differences among people with autism that we need to look closely at each person to understand his or her potential. As you will learn, the individual's personal learning style and physical responses will help us select the best treatment and education.

Are there other differences between people with autism?

Besides the various sensory problems, intelligence levels, and communication abilities, people with autism can show differences in:

A) The age of onset, when the syndrome becomes evident
B) The presence of other health problems like seizure disorders
C) Tendencies to obsessive-compulsive behavior
D) The presence and degree of antisocial behaviors they may exhibit

A) *Age of onset:* A child with a serious form of autism may show signs that we can recognize in early childhood, but usually not before the age of two and a half. Some others with a much milder set of symptoms may not be diagnosed until much later, perhaps as late as the teen years.

B) *Seizure disorders and other health problems:* For reasons not fully understood, 20 to 30 percent of people with autism have some form of seizures during their lifetime, either occurring only in childhood, or enduring into adult life, or suddenly appearing for the first time after adolescence. We don't understand whether the seizures cause the autism, or if the autism causes the seizures. In general, however, people with autism are more likely to have seizures than the general population.

Other unusual biological features appear connected to autism, but we don't understand their significance at this time. For example, a genetic condition called fragile X, (named for the bent, or "fragile" appearance of the X chromosome under magnification) will be discussed in Chapter 4. Doctors initially hoped that the discovery of fragile X would lead to better understanding and prevention of autism. But they soon found that only 15 or 20 percent of the people with autism had this chromosomal disorder, an anomaly that appears even more common among people with more general characteristics of mental retardation.

Taps of spinal fluid show that some people with autism have an abnormally high count of certain neurotransmitters, the fluids in the brain that relay electrical currents from cell to cell. This discovery seemed promising ten years ago but led to no significant treatment. In fact, there's no evidence that these surplus neurotransmitters cause any of the symptoms. These irregularities may coexist with autism without actually affecting the developmental pattern.

Many families believe their child has unusual reactions to certain foods or chemicals and think that allergies might be involved. However, medical research hasn't proved a connection with autism. In some cases, however, the term *autistic* has been misused to describe people with extreme allergies who don't really have the neurological disorder we know as autism.

C) *Obsessive–compulsive behavior:* Many unusual traits have been traced to neurological problems, including strange body movements, problems with concentration, and repetitive behaviors. Some people with autism have difficulty controlling their behavior. They may seem trapped in a habit, insist on following the same routines, or have trouble changing from one subject to another. They may become fanatical collectors of one particular thing or everything, never throwing anything away. However, obsessive–compulsive behavior is not always a sign of autism. It may mean the person has other neurological, biochemical, or psychological problems.

D) *Antisocial behaviors:* Since most people with autism have serious communication problems and limited social skills, it shouldn't surprise us that some have difficult behaviors. Often these behaviors actually serve a functional purpose for the individual, appalling as others may find them. A technique called functional analysis of behavior lets us analyze these behaviors to discover potential meanings behind otherwise meaningless antisocial acts like violence, self-abuse, and withdrawal (see Chapter 11).

We have all experienced a communication failure, either with a faulty phone line, a letter lost in the mail, or indecipherable handwriting. Our own experience shows us how quickly we become frustrated if another person doesn't understand us. That frustration would increase if other people always treated us as if we were stupid, or made all decisions for us and gave us orders we didn't understand.

People with autism often find themselves in a position where they can't negotiate or influence people through words. They are not "smooth talkers." Some learn that if they can't win an argument or get their way through language, they can with behavior.

Sometimes the behaviors shock and alarm other people. Unfortunately, this may make the behavior seem even more effective and desirable to the person with the communication disorder. Unfortunate examples include physical violence (breaking windows or furniture, attacking others), rebellious toilet behavior (refusing to use the toilet, smearing feces on walls, clothing, self), and even self-injury (biting one's hands, head-banging, pinching oneself, tearing at clothing or hair, even gouging at the eyes).

Extreme behavior problems are not the first signs of autism. They generally develop later, after the person becomes frustrated trying and failing to communicate with others and exert some control on the outside world. Ideally, early childhood programs should prevent severe behavior disorders by teaching children acceptable forms of request, refusal, and negotiation. It's always harder to stop a behavior after the person has found it brings gratification (people find it hard to ignore the most abusive behaviors, and generally succumb to another's demands to avoid a tantrum). However, even the most disturbing habits of an older person may yield to good behavioral therapy.

Is each person with autism different?

This is one of the great half-truths that confuses the public about autism and makes many people misunderstand the importance of this label. Some believe that no two people with autism are alike, simply because they haven't seen more than one person with a particular pattern of autism.

In a sense, we could argue that each human on the planet is different, or "one-of-a-kind." Even identical twins, total clones at birth, begin to develop differences as life gives them separate experiences, different medical histories, and memories.

Persons with autism can have more differences among each other than do typical people of their age, sex, and nationality. As already explained, they may score higher or lower than the norm on tests of hearing, touch, etc. However, they share some common learning problems and have difficulties with social development.

If there are so many differences between people with autism, what do they have in common?

Dr. Lorna Wing, a physician in England who is also the mother of a daughter with autism, uses the expression *au-*

tistic triad when writing about three common characteristics of people with this disability. Dr. Wing believes that people with every form and degree of autism share three characteristics: limitations in language, social understanding, and imagination.

Besides the autistic triad, researchers in both England and the United States have noticed other common features of autism:

A) Memory and sense of direction are often stronger than other skills.
B) Understanding time and the order of events is difficult.
C) Thinking is based more on association than reasoning.
D) There is a dependency on routines and resistance to change.
E) Controlling emotion or excitement appears difficult.
F) Habits and interests are often unusual or eccentric.

A) Memory and sense of direction may be better than average. In fact, some people with autism show amazing ability in these areas, even as very young children. Parents have often reported that a child has learned to read just by watching *Sesame Street* or T.V. game shows that feature word puzzles.

Sometimes the memory is used to recall information you and I would ignore or consider unimportant, such as the name of every street along a highway, telephone numbers used years ago, or an entire television schedule.

Many people with autism can recognize the directions to a place they have been only once before. This talent is one of many types of spatial skills. These skills include the ability to recognize a pattern or shape, no matter what position it is in. This talent often shows up in childhood if a child easily puts puzzles together or has no trouble seeing the difference between letters that confuse other children. For example, the average youngster has trouble telling the difference between a *b* and a *d*, or even a *p*. In the first months of writing they often print a few letters backwards, showing the difficulty of learning the correct pattern in space and position. But learners with autism often have superior talent in this area.

The individual's strengths can often make up for other weaknesses or learning problems. If we recognize the learners' talents, we can help them succeed. "Challenge the student's strengths, offer support for his weaknesses," is the motto of many successful teachers.

B) Understanding time and the order of events is very hard for some people with autism. Dr. Eric Schopler, founder of the largest research center for autism in the world, calls this a time perception disorder.

Dr. Schopler has observed that many people with autism have trouble estimating the length of a given time period or understanding which event happened before another one. In other words, time appears unpredictable to them. It may seem to pass unbearably slowly, making the person desperately impatient, or it may speed by unnoticed.

Students with autism often have good memory skills to record information, but can't then organize it into sequence or recognize which of several events came first. It may be hard to understand what we call cause and effect, that one thing happens (*a car slides on wet pavement*) because another thing happened first (*it rained an hour earlier*).

C) Thinking is based more on association than reasoning. The type of thinking we call reasoning depends on our use of concepts like *if* and *then* and *why*, all part of understanding cause and effect. Some people with autism, even those who are highly intelligent, have trouble with reasoning or putting ideas together in order to solve problems.

When a person has trouble understanding the sequence of things, or cause and effect, it makes it very difficult to develop judgment and recognize hazards. Some people with autism don't recognize dangers in everyday situations—speeding traffic, high ladders, or fire hazards. On the other hand, the same individuals might be terrified of totally harmless things like a kitten, a road sign, or even a common food. Parents can only guess the reasons behind their child's irrational fears. The child has probably made a personal association between the object of fear and some earlier, bad experience.

A person who's terrified of pickles probably associates them with an unfortunate incident from the past. Perhaps he once cut his hand while opening a jar of pickles. That experience wouldn't make a typical person fear pickles forever. The average person's reasoning ability tells him or her to be more careful with glass jars. But a person with autism, who has difficulty comprehending cause and effect, may draw another conclusion. "Pickles are dangerous. They can make you cut your hand."

We can't read the minds of others just by watching their behavior, but professionals have always considered unusual fears a key sign of autism. *Irrational fears* and *indifference to danger* are two of the terms used to describe the symptoms since the 1940s. We seem closer to understanding this now, but the mystery remains as long as people with autism can't explain their personal fears.

D) *There is a dependency on routines.* When people have trouble reasoning, or making decisions, it's very tempting to rely on habit. People with autism often show this tendency to follow routine. Some individuals, for instance, appear confused and easily upset by changes in their schedules. They may insist on always following the same routines and order, putting every object in a precise place or position, perhaps even dressing the same way every day.

The routines may become so important to the person that he or she cannot function without the familiar signals or directions used by a parent or teacher. Sometimes a person with autism won't act independently and needs instructions such as "get up," "sit down," "eat your breakfast."

This behavior is called prompt dependency, because the person depends on prompts to do simple, familiar tasks. We also use the term *cue bound*, meaning a person's behavior is tied to a familiar cue.

Autism may make a person appear stubborn or unwilling to try anything new. However, resistance to change may be the person's only way to cope. Perhaps changes in the environment would be too confusing and frightening for a person who has trouble processing information from the different senses of sight, sound, touch, and so on. Routines and familiar cues may offer comfort, order that the individual has come to understand and expect.

E) Controlling emotion or excitement is difficult. People with autism often have trouble lowering their level of excitement or emotion, a process sometimes called down-regulating. Children with neurological problems often show problems coping with stress or distractions.

Dr. Eric Courchesne, noted for his research with magnetic resonance imaging, believes people with autism have neurological problems that make it hard to regulate attention, to change their focus at will, or to respond to new stimuli. Simply put, these people have less choice or control over their perspective. Most of us have the ability to change our frame of mind, to put one thought "on hold" while another demands our attention. After the brief distraction (an auto honking, a neighbor waving across the fence, or a fly buzzing near our head), we can reshift our attention, often without missing a word in our conversation. Courchesne warns us that people with autism face a double disadvantage: they may find it hard to respond to the distracting stimulus (a ringing phone, a changing traffic light, the smell of cookies baking), but once distracted, they may become so preoccupied with the stimulus they have trouble returning their attention to an earlier activity, such as work, conversation, or even play. When this type of child gets upset, the parents have trouble getting him to calm down, shift his attention, or change to another subject.

Most of us have occasional problems controlling our feelings or calming ourselves. Though we usually develop more self-control as we mature, adults with autism generally have problems in this area, remaining overly excitable. Even Temple Grandin, a woman accomplished enough to write the first autobiographical account of autism, admits she has problems controlling her emotions under pressure. In *Emergence, Labeled Autistic*, Grandin explains that she hasn't overcome her neurological problems, but has adopted rules that let her succeed in spite of her autism.

Grandin won't express anger or criticism in writing, because it may be held against her. She'll use the phone instead. If she feels she's losing control on the phone, she'll quickly terminate the conversation with as much courtesy as she can muster. Finally, she avoids unnecessary conflicts, like meetings she won't enjoy and relationships that seem threatening.

Grandin's rules make sense, not just for her, but for everyone. Instead of expecting our children to overcome the challenges of autism, we should follow Temple's example, set reasonable boundaries for behavior and try to minimize stress in the environment.

F) *Habits and interests are often unusual or eccentric.* Unusual habits and interests don't necessarily indicate autism. Our culture tolerates, even encourages, individuality. However, people with autism often have hobbies or pastimes that stand out as eccentric and bizarre.

Even the most capable people with autism seem to march to a different drummer. Their selection of clothing, conversation, and recreation tend to be highly individual, not following the general fashions or fads. Examples might include obsessive collections that no one else understands, such as photographs of traffic lights, vintage adding machines, or ketchup bottles.

People with autism may choose an unusual style of clothing. Perhaps an individual will wear the same color every day, or put on unseasonal clothing such as short pants during winter, or wear gloves and overcoat into late spring.

These personal choices might seem unsuitable or even

annoying to others, but this doesn't necessarily concern the person with autism, who probably doesn't even pay attention to other people's taste. Most people with autism are blissfully unaware that other human beings may be viewing them, or judging their appearance. The individual is more likely to care about personal freedom—his right to choose his clothing and her right to pick her hairstyle.

Naturally, parents want their child to appear as normal and attractive as possible, but they should avoid unnecessary battles over grooming and clothing selection. As long as your child meets community standards of decency and hygiene, everything else should be negotiable. The freedom to choose one's apparel can be a powerful motivator for a person who has limited opportunities for personal expression.

Creative parents can use the wardrobe as a method for negotiating around other behaviors. For example, one mother bought her six-year-old daughter an array of flowered panties, showed them to the girl, and said, "When you go potty by yourself, we can throw away those diapers and you can wear these." It worked. Within two days the girl was toilet trained. Sometimes, however, an individual will insist on inappropriate clothing choices, so the parents have to negotiate around that unfortunate fixation. The child simply cannot wear the same shirt everyday, but Mom might agree to buy three identical ones, so one is always clean and ready to put on. The young woman can't go out of the house wearing her brassiere outside of her sweater like Madonna, but she can dress that way around the house. The possibilities for negotiation are limitless, and give your child the sense that he has control of his life. A pierced ear, a tattered coat, or a vulgar T-shirt is a small price to pay for your daughter's or son's self-esteem.

Does autism affect females differently than males?

For reasons not yet understood, autism affects about four times as many males as females. This statistic has puzzled researchers since doctors first began using the word *autism*.

Today specialists are paying more attention to the differences among people with autism and looking for subtypes.

In 1966 Dr. Andreas Rett made a sudden discovery at his clinic in Vienna. By chance, two girls were awaiting their appointments in the same reception area. They had striking similarities that inspired the doctor to research other cases that might indicate a specific syndrome. He discovered an unusual form of autism that seemed to affect only girls. That subtype is now called Rett syndrome. Eventually a few males were diagnosed with Rett syndrome, but the overwhelming majority of affected individuals are female. See Chapter 4 for more information about different forms of autism.

Perhaps research will discover subtypes of autism that only affect males. That might explain the difference between the number of girls and boys with the general diagnosis. However, at this time there is no evidence that females have a different form of autism than males. Both males and females are found in every level of ability within the category of autism.

Do people with autism live in a "world of their own"?

You may have heard people use phrases like "behind a wall," "in a shell," or "shutting the world out" to describe people with autism. These expressions don't really describe the experience of the person with autism. They only describe the first impressions of people who haven't learned the real nature of autism.

Before psychiatrists understood the neurological nature of autism, they thought the patients had escaped into their minds to shut out the world. That theory has been disproven, but many people still speak in those terms. Why? Because the gestures and appearance of people with autism *look* like escapism and isolation. Many avoid eye contact, because they don't recognize subtle signals of interest or attention in the gaze of others. If we had visual processing problems, we might ignore eye contact too.

We no longer believe that individuals with autism would be like typical people if they just came out of their shell or out from behind their wall. Their neurological differences will endure, but they share our basic human instincts, seeking pleasure and avoiding discomfort or boredom. The trouble is, our social customs have developed around the convenience of the typical person, and may not suit people with exceptional neurological systems.

Do they make friends or care about people?

One of the sadder misunderstandings regarding autism is that individuals with the disorder can't feel love or show it, that it is somehow not a part of their physical or emotional world. This is just not true.

Many people use the expression *universal language of love* to describe a group of natural, spontaneous behaviors including smiles, caresses, soft words, and other gestures that mean "love" in any culture or country, no matter what language the people speak. Of course, many people with autism don't use such gestures to express affection, for their neurological differences keep them from mastering the universal language of love. That doesn't mean they don't love; they just can't express their feelings in a way that we always recognize.

Most parents know from their own experience that their child with autism has feelings and preferences for other people, including loyalties to their family. However, problems of expression keep them from making the typical gestures of love and friendship. Naturally, family members look for responsive signs of affection. When they can't recognize those feelings in their child's gestures, the parents' disappointment can lead to discouragement. This may make the child with autism even more confused and frustrated. She probably expects her parents to understand that she's been loving the only way she knows how.

Any of us would seem withdrawn or indifferent if we couldn't master the language of love. If we consistently failed to respond to others on cue, they might quit offering us smiles and salutations. If others ignored our forms of greeting, we'd give up trying to reach them. Behind the subtle differences of eye contact and gesture, there's always a human being, more like us than different.

Are real people with autism like the ones shown in movies or on TV?

Unless you have seen interviews with individuals who have autism, or watched a documentary made to train parents and professionals, you probably haven't seen a reliable picture of this disability. Television shows aim to entertain more than to educate. Even the programs that begin with a true-life story exaggerate and manipulate to capture our attention. Film producers want the biggest audience possible, so they seek out the unusual and then stress its sensational side.

Rain Man, starring Dustin Hoffman as a middle-aged man with autism, stands out as one of the most realistic pictures of this disability. Hoffman plays an "autistic savant," a very rare type of person with a remarkable combination of genius in some skills and total incapacity in others. He amazes audiences with his mathematical ability, yet he doesn't know whether a car costs more than a candy bar. Although it's hard to believe, a small number of people with autism actually resemble this portrait. However, the movie stages some unlikely plot twists for the sake of entertainment.

Most Hollywood films exploit misunderstandings about autism for dramatic value. For example, *The Boy Who Could Fly* shows a teenaged boy with autism literally fly away from an institution. He sweeps and soars over roof-

tops like Mary Poppins. His miracle inspires other characters to solve their personal problems and look forward to a
happy ending. Unfortunately, it's not a happy ending for
those who want the public to understand autism.

REVIEW

There are tremendous variations between people with autism. For this reason, we cannot describe a "typical" example or stereotype. There are simply too many levels of
intelligence and language, too many behaviors and personal
habits to give us a standard portrait of people within this
group.

Key signs of autism include unusual responses to the five
senses, uneven performance on intelligence tests, communication problems, and poor social skills. Yet, there is room
for individual exceptions within each of these shared
symptoms.

The variety of behaviors, talents, and problems makes it
hard to recognize that two very different persons may both
have autism. However, research over the years has shown
some fairly predictable learning patterns such as strength
in spatial skills and memory and weakness in language and
reasoning ability.

People with neurological differences, such as those caused
by autism, may find some of our activities (especially those
that involve complicated social responses) meaningless, unpredictable, even disturbing. As a result they may choose
to avoid social contact, or even develop behaviors we call
antisocial.

What else should we read?

Greenfield, Josh. *A Child Called Noah.* New York: Holt,
Rinehart and Winston, 1971. A father writes about the unusual development of his second son, and the search for a
diagnosis and treatment.

What Are People with Autism Like?

Hart, Charles A. *Without Reason: A Family Copes with Two Generations of Autism.* New York: Harper & Row, 1989. This book reveals the author's experience with autism, first in an older brother and later in his own son.

Kaufman, Barry. *Son-Rise.* New York: Harper & Row, 1976. Also widely aired on television, the story of the Kaufman family tells how they identified their son's autism, subsequently confirmed by professional diagnosis, and developed an innovative form of imitation therapy to help him.

Park, Clara Claiborn. *The Siege.* New York: Harcourt Brace Jovanovich, 1967. The author describes the experience of raising a daughter with autism and the family's never-ending search for answers.

3

What Causes
Autism?

Autism is not due to neglect, abuse or tragedy, all causes long since disproved by professionals. Unfortunately, the general understanding of the word autistic hasn't kept up with medical research.

The mystery of autism always returns to the same question: What causes this strange disorder? Parents ask, "How can a person who looks just like me behave so strangely? If my child can see and hear, why doesn't he pay attention? How can she seem so bright at some moments and completely incapable at others?"

The professionals who named autism were trained in the theories of Sigmund Freud, the father of psychoanalysis. In the 1940s through the 1960s, Freud's beliefs had a strong influence on the field we call behavioral sciences. His followers tried to explain every manner of human behavior in terms of early childhood experience. They thought, for example, that the first months of life were the single most important determinants of the individual's later personality, talents, in short, his or her destiny.

It would be many years before scientists discovered some of the biochemical and physical causes of certain types of behavior. Doctors, following the theories of their time, believed that autism had been caused by unfortunate childhood experiences, tragedy, or neglect. Unfortunately, some people still believe this naive and primitive theory.

Is autism caused by the parents, and could they have done anything to prevent it?

The answers to these often asked questions are "No!" and "No!" Research hasn't fully explained the causes of autism, but this question has been answered again and again. There is absolutely nothing a parent can do, either deliberately or unconsciously, to cause this neurological disorder in a child.

For years, psychoanalysts and psychologists tried to find a pattern in family life to explain the cause of autism or design a treatment to cure it. Yet most families with such a child also raised other sons or daughters who had typical developmental patterns. Today we know that this is one more proof that a mother or father cannot cause autism; the way parents treated an affected child did nothing to make him or her develop differently than the nondisabled children in the family.

Autism appears in families of every type, rich and poor, lower class and upper class, rural and urban. Autism appears in children of every ethnic and cultural group across the globe. However, children in wealthier nations are more likely to be diagnosed and given early assistance than those in poorer countries. People with autism, like those with other disabilities, need services and trained professionals unavailable in poor societies.

In 1971 Dr. Bernard Rimland, a psychologist whose son had autism, published *Infantile Autism,* a landmark book for the times. Following the example set by Dr. Lorna Wing in England, Dr. Rimland helped organize a National Society for Autistic Citizens (NSAC) in the United States. This organization encouraged professionals to quit blaming parents for their child's autism.

At the same time, Drs. Robert Reichler and Eric Schopler

founded a research and clinical center at the University of North Carolina (Division TEACCH) that would influence thinking about autism throughout the world.

This new generation of psychiatrists and psychologists believed that parents were not the problem, or "cause" of autism. Rather, they believed that parents were potential partners in treatment, cotherapists who deserved support, not blame.

Do we understand the causes of autism better now than in the past?

Throughout history, theories about the mind have been just that—theories with very little proof or evidence to back them up. Until recently, no one could examine the brains of living subjects or even measure the electrical impulses that form the majority of communication within the brain.

Modern technology lets doctors recognize subtle differences in the blood, spinal fluid, and chromosomes of people. It's also possible to measure the amount of electrical activity in different parts of the brain during thought processes. These medical discoveries let us understand the mind better than we did in the past.

Today doctors recognize that differences in thought and behavior can have many causes. It will take more research before we answer all of our questions about autism, but scientists are still exploring the effects of biology and genetics on behavior.

Dr. Edward Ritvo has reported research on forty pairs of twins affected by autism, including twenty-three sets of identical twins and seventeen sets of fraternal twins. Ritvo hoped to determine whether their autism was due to genetics or some disease during fetal development.

Identical twins are biological clones, sharing the same biological qualities, including finger prints. If autism were caused simply by genetics, each identical twin would have the same neurological structure. Either both would have autism, or neither would be affected. On the other hand, fraternal twins have different genetic programs. They've shared the womb for nine months, but their genes can be as different as any brother's or sister's. If the two genetically different twins both develop autism, it suggests an environmental cause; perhaps a virus infected the mother during pregnancy, or she was exposed to a chemical pollutant.

As Ritvo expected, he found the strongest similarities between identical twins. In twenty-two of these twenty-three sets of identical twins, both had autism and developed in very similar patterns. The fraternal twins showed fewer similarities. In several pairs, one child showed typical development in spite of having a twin disabled with autism.

The real surprise in Ritvo's research concerns the set of identical twins who didn't share developmental qualities: one clearly had autism, the other didn't. This research suggests an interesting possibility. Perhaps autism is not purely genetic. Rather, autism may require some disease-borne or chemical trauma to a developing fetus as a precipitating factor. Perhaps the pregnant mother contracts rubella, or another illness that affects her unborn child. Maybe industrial pollution affects the developing fetus.

Maybe autism cannot be inherited, but the susceptibility to autism might plague some families, just as cancer runs in families. Cancer is usually triggered by the environment (too much sun, tobacco smoke, carcinogens in the food) yet research documents that some families have a higher rate of response to these environmental hazards than the average.

Science doesn't have all the answers yet, but the set of identical twins who don't share autism poses the question, Is autism caused by a combination of genetics and disease? Perhaps the identical twins shared a genetic weakness making them susceptible to prenatal damage. When a viral or toxic substance entered their mother's womb, it affected one child, but missed the other.

Is autism caused by a disease?

Autism is not a disease that infects an infant or child after birth like mumps or measles. Rather, that child's developmental problems begin with neurological differences that start in the womb, though we might not recognize the symptoms for years. Microscopic studies of the brains of people with autism don't show specific areas of damaged or dead cells, like those caused by lack of oxygen or brain injury. They show unusual growth patterns, probably beginning in the first six months of pregnancy.

Some diseases, such as rubella (German measles), create risks of developmental disabilities for unborn children. If a pregnant woman is exposed to some disease-bearing substances, germs, viruses, or dangerous chemicals, her unborn child may be affected. At this time, however, no disease or hazardous substance is known to be the sole cause of autism. In fact, some medical researchers believe that the pregnant woman's health is only one of many factors that could result in autism.

If autism is a birth defect, why does it take years for the effects to show up?

Generally, we expect birth defects to show up while the doctors give the newborn the first examination. Even some forms of mental retardation, such as Down syndrome and other chromosomal disorders, leave telltale signs in the blood or urine. In fact, amniocentesis, the test of amniotic fluid surrounding a child in the womb, can indicate many forms of disability even before birth. However, modern medicine has as yet discovered no certain chemical or chromosomal tests to predict autism.

Autism is considered a developmental disability with no known physical markers, meaning that no physical signs, either obvious to the naked eye or emerging after sophisticated laboratory testing, reveal the condition.

We still don't know which effects of autism to call "primary" and which to call "secondary." The primary effects occur between conception and birth, and the secondary effects follow birth. Neurologists realize that the brain continues to grow after birth, following that genetic or organic pattern. But other factors—nutrition; exercise; physical, sensory, and intellectual stimulation—can also affect the growth of the brain.

Some people look at autism strictly from a behavioral point of view. They say that autism isn't present until the child exhibits the telltale behaviors. This raises another riddle about autism: Can a nonverbal baby have autism? Or do we have to wait until the child is a nonverbal three-year-old to say he has this symptom of autism? The answer is, autism is a developmental disability whose symptoms only show up in the course of development, not at any one point in time, especially not at birth.

What's the difference between autism and mental illness?

Medical terms sometimes have a shadowy and uncertain history. The original purpose of the term *mental illness* was to suggest a difference between diseases of the body and diseases of the mind. But medical research has been showing closer and closer ties between disorders of both mind and body. For example, many diseases labeled psychoses or other forms of mental illness respond better to physical treatment (prescription medicines) than predicted a generation ago when psychiatrists believed "talking" therapies could cure. Where therapy has failed, medication often succeeds.

Psychiatrists now understand the biology and medical problems of their patients better than in the past. Differences in human behavior and attitude are no longer explained simply in terms of Freudian theory and early childhood experiences. Behavioral science is becoming more like the other branches of medicine, and mental problems are seen as having physical causes in many cases.

Autism appears at a different age than mental illness. We usually recognize autism at the age of thirty to thirty-six months. Severely disabled children may show symptoms earlier, and marginal cases can escape diagnosis until the early teens. In contrast, mental illness usually doesn't appear during childhood. Schizophrenia and bipolar disorders surface in the late teens or early adult years.

From a medical perspective, there are other, more important differences between autism and mental illness. Autism has more to do with the brain's structure than its chemistry. It's not caused by chemical variations in the brain, nor will it respond to drugs designed for psychotic patients. The drug may slow down or sedate a person with autism, but not improve her or his thought processes.

Mental illness appears more sporadic, characterized by wide mood swings caused by cyclical changes in the amount of certain chemicals produced in the brain. These chemicals are called neurotransmitters, and they are responsible for the transfer of neuro signals from one part of the brain to another; when production of one or several substances goes out of balance, a necessary neurotransmitter can't function and others dominate. This may cause dramatic mood swings, or periods of fantasy and delusion. During psychotic episodes, some mental patients act out bizarre behaviors. These are often unpredictable and temporary personality changes, totally out of character with the person's regular temperament.

Without medication to control an abnormal level of neurotransmitters, a person with mental illness may experience ups and downs, sometimes growing worse with time. In contrast, the individual with autism always has her or his unusual neurological patterns. Many forms of mental illness respond to "chemical cures" (drugs that regulate a temporary imbalance of neurotransmitters). However, those medications don't work as well with autism. Drugs simply don't reroute a person's neurological pathways or create new brain cells.

Is autism inherited? Does autism occur more often in some families than in the rest of the population?

The question of heredity and family medical history is never easy to answer. Few human conditions are totally predictable just by looking at the characteristics of the mother and father. Some physical qualities, such as coloring and bone structure, often show up in our offspring. However, many genetic tendencies appear to skip a generation or disappear entirely if diet or life-style changes after a few generations.

Autism is called a low-incidence disability, because it affects such a small percentage of people. Unlike blue eyes or curly hair, which offers unlimited numbers of subjects to study, autism doesn't provide many examples for genetic research.

In the early 1980s the first serious study of family patterns of autism began at UCLA. Dr. Edward Ritvo advertised nationally to find families that had more than one diagnosed case of autism, either within one generation (brothers, sisters, cousins) or across generations (parents/children, aunts/nieces). This first study identified less than one hundred families with second or third incidences of autism.

A few years later Dr. Ritvo helped the University of Utah conduct a state-wide search for families with a reoccurrence of autism in that state. The Mormon church cooperated in the research, allowing the researchers to use the church's extensive records of family histories going back many generations. This study uncovered some amazing case studies. Many families could report cousins, nieces, nephews, aunts, and uncles with the disability. One family had five children, all with the diagnosis of autism. This family's experience suggests a strong genetic factor may be passed along by parents who show no trace of the disability themselves.

Because of the social awkwardness usually found in autism, people with the diagnosis are less likely to marry than the general population. However, researchers in the Utah study found eleven autistic adults who had not only married, but had offspring of their own.

The eleven adults in this study represented ten married couples. Nine of them had married nonautistic partners, and two had married each other. Together, these ten couples had forty-four children. Twenty of them, or 46 percent, had autism! This study from the *American Journal of Psychiatry* (February, 1989) clearly demonstrates that autism has a genetic, or hereditary, factor.

Critics complain that this study may have reported too high a rate of genetic influence because the researchers focused their attention on families that already had identified more than one case of autism. Skeptics claim that families with only one incidence of autism were ignored or overlooked by this study. Later studies will try to examine a larger cross section of the public to determine how often autism occurs in families with no previous history of the disorder.

Research on this topic continues, both in Great Britain and at Stanford University. Before long we may have more information about family patterns of autism to compare with the earlier study.

The next logical questions following this thinking are obvious. If autism is hereditary, who carries the gene? and Why doesn't it show up more often, if all the brothers and sisters carry the genes to their children? Today we simply don't yet have the answers to these questions. We can only guess by looking at the hereditary patterns of other conditions.

For years genetic researchers have known that some genetic conditions, such as hemophilia, cystic fibrosis, and one form of muscular dystrophy, are passed along by carriers who don't have the disease. Often the parents who pass on the gene causing the disability don't know they have the genetic trait until they have an affected child. It appears that a person may carry a gene that potentially causes autism, but the disorder won't occur unless there's another factor, such as the other parent's genetic influence, or some disease or environmental pollutant.

A great deal of medical research now concentrates on finding the location of the specific genes that cause inherited conditions. However, geneticists haven't found any markers that show exactly which gene(s) may cause autism or transmit the genetic trait to future offspring.

Heredity raises another important question about autism: Do specific genes cause autism? Or do these genes simply interfere with the embryo's immune system, so that a disease may cause autism?

We now know that many conditions "run in families" but only appear after an individual is exposed to a virus, a chemical, or another environmental factor that triggers it. Research shows that some families have a much higher rate of cancer than other families exposed to the same hazards. Yet it is the environmental hazard (x-ray exposure, pollution, etc.) that causes the disease. The families' genes only pass along a weakness or vulnerability.

The same issue of vulnerability may help explain the genetic pattern in autism. Family groups may pass along the tendency, but no individual will show the disorder until he or she comes in contact with the triggering substance. Studies indicate that this is the case with alcoholism. The trait may pass from generation to generation, but no one will become an alcoholic without using alcohol.

Since we haven't found genetic markers for autism, some questions remain unanswered. Ritvo's study of the twins raised the issue of genetic vulnerability in autism. The pair of identical twins who didn't share autism demonstrates that the affected twin's disability couldn't have been merely genetic. Yet the co-occurrence in the other twenty-two pairs of identical twins shows a powerful genetic factor.

Researchers call conditions that show hereditary as well as environmental factors syndromes. For example, high blood pressure is called a medical syndrome because it's effected by genealogy, diet, and stress, not just a single cause. Accordingly, many professionals use the term *autistic syndrome* when discussing the biology and causes of this disorder.

Can neglect, abuse, or tragedy make a person autistic?

The word *autistic* has entered our language and taken on meanings that have little to do with the developmental disability we call autism. In the first few decades that psychiatrists believed autism was caused by the patient's withdrawal from other people, they used the term freely to describe behaviors of other people who seemed antisocial or self-absorbed. Unfortunately, nonprofessionals and amateur psychologists adopted the label, lending it a misleading conversational meaning.

The way people respond to neglect, abuse, or sorrow may resemble some of the symptoms of autism. For example, a neglected child may be slow to speak. Abuse could teach fear of contact with others. Sorrow or tragedy can make a person withdraw from friends or family. But none of those experiences can cause the neurological disorder, the developmental disability, that the professional community knows as autism.

Autism is *not* caused by neglect, abuse, or tragedy. Unfortunately, the general understanding of the word *autistic* hasn't kept up with medical research.

Is autism caused by modern life-styles, diet, or pollution?

Modern technology and our changing life-styles have affected our environment and the health of many individuals. Scientists have discovered new problems brought about by the use of detergents, insecticides, herbicides, and other substances that contribute to pollution. In industrialized countries we even eat a diet unlike our ancestors, raising many questions about the long-term effects on health. No wonder that doctors occasionally announce the discovery of a new disease or health hazard.

Possibly we will discover that some of our new chemical products and pollutants increase the rate of all birth defects, including autism. However, we have other evidence to show that this disability isn't new at all, only newly named and recognized.

In *Autism: Explaining the Enigma,* Uta Frith writes about the lives of historical figures who meet today's definition of autism. From evidence like this and other sources, we have reason to believe that this disability has been part of human experience for ages. The "wise fools" in the Middle Ages and the "changeling children" of folklore may have had autism. Furthermore, we see cases of autism in the most underdeveloped nations, not just those affected by modern technology.

Do people make themselves autistic? Do they choose to live in their "own world"?

The first theory of autism suggested that the person with autism shut out the world as a defense against unpleasant experiences, or to turn away from a cold, "refrigerator" mother. By the late 1960s, researchers no longer accepted that opinion. But they still had no information about the biological causes of the disability.

Before the discovery of neurological evidence, many authorities focused on the behavioral symptoms of autism to explain its cause. They suggested that the behavior itself made the person autistic. In other words, the child is autistic because he *behaves* autistically! People who believed this thought they could "cure" the person by eliminating autistic behaviors.

If behavior alone makes the person autistic, and changing

the behavior makes them nonautistic, then it might seem that people are responsible for their condition. But, are they autistic because they choose to practice abnormal habits, use unusual gestures, and refuse to cooperate? Probably not.

The behavioral view of autism ignores the many steps of neuromotor activity needed to complete a behavior. Blaming autism on the behavior may make a parent overlook the complicated nature of the child's performance.

Parents and teachers often try to control a behavior by removing distractions and directing the student's attention to details or rewards. But they may not recognize the particular learner's challenge. Repeating or shouting instructions won't help a child who can't process audial information. The learner's responses still depend on his or her own mental and physical reflexes.

Some behaviors, such as poor eye contact, are called symptoms of autism. But labeling the behavior a symptom isn't the same as understanding the behavior.

Most people use eye contact to draw and hold the attention of others. Infants use eye contact as one of the first steps in communication: when the mother averts her gaze, the child looks to see the direction of mother's attention. Children learn to measure peoples' interest, pleasure, or disapproval by eye contact.

Looking into another person's eyes is a natural and spontaneous gesture for most people ... because they find it useful! But a person who can't recognize details of facial expression, or who has a delayed response to images, may never recognize the relationship between another person's gaze and the events around them. When neurological differences interfere with timing or direction, an individual misses the subtle coordination of gestures between speaker and listener. Eye contact might be taught as a learned behavior, but, if it isn't spontaneous, it may not prove useful or informative to the student.

Researchers are working to map the neurological paths of stimulus and response; sensation, thought, and action. They've already discovered differences between people with autism and those without. We don't have explanations for these differences yet, but it's become clear that people don't make themselves autistic by choosing autistic behaviors. Choice has nothing to do with it. They're showing us that their minds and bodies are wired a little differently than the average person's. (See Chapter 9.)

REVIEW

Over the years many theories have been offered about the causes of autism. Before modern research, psychiatrists believed that the disorder was caused by psychological problems, perhaps bad parenting. This theory has been totally disproven by later biological studies.

Although we seem closer to understanding the cause of autism than in the past, researchers think it may depend on a number of factors. They don't call it a disease, in the sense that a child becomes infected after birth. However, a pregnant mother's disease (such as rubella measles) may be a factor causing autism. If the mother is infected during a critical period of pregnancy, it may effect her child's neurological development.

We believe the syndrome of autism probably begins before birth. That's why it's considered a congenital birth defect. However, the symptoms usually aren't noticeable for many months, even years. No one can detect the disorder until the child shows delays or disturbance of development. Accordingly, we call it a developmental disability.

Autism differs from mental illness in many ways: Symptoms appear earlier in life. Autism involves neurological differences, not just variations of brain chemicals. Finally, it won't respond to the treatments for psychotic disorders.

A growing body of research shows that some families have a higher risk of autism than the general public. However, no racial or ethnic group appears to have a greater incidence of autism than others.

Autism is not a new human condition brought about by the stress or pollution of modern society. It occurs in rural, undeveloped societies as well as in highly industrialized ones. A review of historical biographies suggests that there were people with autism long before we had a word for their condition.

People do not make themselves autistic. They do not choose to withdraw from the world of others, nor do they work themselves into a trance with unusual behaviors. Their behaviors are the result, not the cause, of unusual neuromotor patterns.

What else should I read?

Cohen, Donald J., Donnelan, A., and Paul, R., eds. *Handbook of Autism and Pervasive Developmental Disorders.* New York: Wiley, 1987.

Coleman, Mary, and Gillberg, Christopher. *The Biology of the Autistic Syndrome.* New York: Praeger, 1985.

Frith, Uta. *Autism: Explaining the Enigma.* Cambridge, MA: Blackwell Pub., 1989. Frith reports life stories from history of unusual people who became legends in their time because of strange behaviors. The author suggests that these individuals might be better understood today through the diagnosis of autism.

Ritvo, Edward. "Concordance of Autism in Forty Pairs of Afflicted Twins." *American Journal of Psychiatry,* Vol. 142, No. 1 (Jan. 1985).

————, et al. "The UCLA–University of Utah Epidemiological Survey of Autism Prevalence," *American Journal of Psychiatry,* Vol. 146, No. 2 (Feb. 1989).

4

Is There More Than One Type of Autism?

The unseen differences between peoples' neuromotor patterns are the secrets behind their developmental problems. Those differences matter more than the behaviors we currently notice and use to classify subgroups today.

We have known from the first published research that people with autism aren't all alike. Anyone who has seen several people with this diagnosis will tell you there is no standard "type." Even the authorities, however, haven't been able to agree on a classification system that makes meaningful distinctions between smaller subtypes. If, and when, we learn to recognize differences based on learning styles and developmental patterns, we will be able to serve individuals better.

While it's easy to say that there are different types, it's much harder to say how many types there are, how we can recognize them, and what makes a particular type different from another.

Progress in this field depends on our ability to classify and recognize subtypes. We need to notice the differences and the similarities between individuals in order to match each person with the most effective education and habilitation services.

In the last twenty years research has shown many different biological problems that affect some, but not all, people with autism. For example, 20 to 30 percent will have a pattern of seizures some time during their lives. These seizures can vary from a mild neurological disorder, detectable only during an electroencephalogram, or a violent seizure involving involuntary movement, loss of consciousness, and high fever. Some people with autism never speak, while others are capable of near-normal conversation. Another type has typical language development until the age of eighteen to twenty-four months but loses all speech afterwards.

Sometimes a medical discovery makes doctors reexamine their earlier beliefs and even change the name of a particular condition. For example, a few years ago physicians recognized a special category of girls who were labeled autistic but had developmental patterns unlike any others. They coined a new name, Rett syndrome, for this disorder, and no longer classify children with this condition under the label *autism*.

Psychologists still have a lot to learn about the developmental and biological differences of subgroups. The breakthrough for people with autism came when professionals stopped calling them schizophrenic or retarded. The first label, *autism*, helped us recognize the qualities that set these people apart from those with other mental disabilities.

Fifty years after this first discovery, it's time to look at the different categories in autism or "the autistic spectrum."

Are there different names for this condition?

There are many terms used by different professionals, but most have nothing to do with the issue of subtypes. Parents may hear more than one diagnosis of the same child: autistic-like, retarded with autistic characteristics, recovered autistic, and residual autism. These labels don't describe differences between the children as much as they indicate differences between the professionals' training and vocabulary.

Only a few forms of autism are known by special terms; Asperger's syndrome—an exceptionally mild case of social impairment and clumsiness—Rett syndrome, and fragile X syndrome are well recognized, but they account for only a small percentage of the group. Professionals often use modifiers like *verbal, nonverbal, high-functioning,* or *low-functioning* to describe different individuals.

What is a subtype anyway?

Recognizing boundaries between individuals or groups is a question of semantics as well as a matter of scientific judgment. The steak one person calls rare will look medium to another. How tall does a dog have to grow before we call it large or how small to be called miniature? Classification systems based on personal judgments aren't very helpful for scientific research.

Scientists look for boundaries between species or qualities to advance their understanding of nature. But researchers don't always agree on the boundary point(s). For example, alchemists believed there were only four elements: fire, air, earth, and water. Science couldn't advance until chemists developed a new classification system, one that recognized more than a hundred elements, each with separate qualities. The improved classification system suddenly made the world more predictable and its elements more manageable in the laboratory.

Some fields of biology have discovered obvious subtypes. Laboratories can recognize subtypes of blood, tissue, hair, neurotransmitters, and even chromosomes. When differences show up under the microscope, that visible evidence lets the biologist identify the subtype. Subtypes of developmental or behavioral disorders don't always have clues that we can recognize in a laboratory specimen.

The behavioral scientists have a harder time discovering subtypes. They can't classify on the basis of a single test at one point in time. Their subject of interest is *behaving*, moving, changing in time.

How can you recognize the different subtypes?

Today, we recognize biological cues for only two of the subtypes:

A) Rett syndrome
B) Fragile X

A) *Rett syndrome:* Specialists no longer consider this a subtype of autism because of dramatic features that make it unlike any other developmental pattern. However, children with this disability are often called autistic during one phase of their illness.

Researchers first believed that Rett syndrome affected only girls until they discovered a few male patients. Still, the overwhelming majority are female and all these children have a specific disorder that grows worse and eventually causes death. These youngsters develop like typical children until around the age of eighteen months, when they start losing motor control.

During the first stage of this disease, patients become awkward, lose the use of their hands, and make repetitive hand movements. They may quit speaking or making eye contact. They show less interest in their environment, making them appear like many children with autism.

As Rett syndrome progresses, the autistic symptoms become less noticeable. However, motor skills get worse. These children need intensive physical therapy. Otherwise, they lose all control of hand movements and cannot even feed themselves. Left alone, they will spend more and more time curled up in a fetal position. Many die in their teens.

B) Fragile X: This syndrome, discovered in 1979, is named for the distinctive appearance of a broken, or "fragile," X chromosome. Fragile X has a unique advantage among subtypes. Any medical laboratory can identify this disorder merely by looking for the chromosomal defect in a blood or tissue sample.

A considerable number of people with autism (perhaps 10 to 20 percent) have fragile X syndrome. But fragile X can also appear in people with mental retardation and no symptoms of autism. Researchers consider this syndrome the second most common form of genetically caused mental retardation.

People with fragile X condition have common physical traits including a high arched palate, problems with teeth alignment, and squinting eyes. Ears are often prominent and set lower than average. Also, males with fragile X syndrome have testicles noticeably larger than normal. It's not necessary for all these symptoms to appear in order to diagnose fragile X syndrome, for a simple laboratory test will show whether the X chromosome has the telltale pattern.

Unfortunately, no other subtype of autism has a detectable physical sign that we're presently able to recognize. We suspect that there are other biologically based subtypes but haven't yet discovered the biological evidence. Hopefully, new medical discoveries will make subtyping easier in the future.

Without clear medical evidence, it's hard to get agreement on the number or nature of subtypes. Ideally, a subtype should have the following qualities:

A) An obvious sign, or "marker," that shows up during an exam or laboratory test
B) A clear boundary between "yes" and "no," so that no examiner would say "maybe," "more," or "less"

C) Early identification, so parents wouldn't be told to "come back in a year or two"
D) Reliable prediction of how an individual will respond to different treatments; which to try and which to avoid

How many subtypes are there?

We don't have biological tests for the different developmental patterns in autism, and thus various experts have different opinions about the number of subtypes. In other words, the answer you hear will depend on who you talk to. Some say there are no subtypes, because people with autism have common problems that overshadow any of their differences.

Many people use the terms *low-functioning* and *high-functioning* when discussing autism. But those categories don't have clear boundaries. While it's easy to say that a nonverbal, apparently retarded, and self-abusive person is low-functioning and one with language and mathematic skills is high-functioning, most people don't fit either the higher or lower extremes of the autistic spectrum. The majority fall somewhere in between with a combination of both low- and high-functioning skills.

There is often disagreement about which label to apply to an individual. A teacher might call her student high-functioning because he performs at grade level or higher in reading and math. But the same student might be called low-functioning by the playground supervisor who observes self-abuse or antisocial behavior. Another child might exhibit a very different, but equally uneven, developmental pattern, showing extreme delay in academic skills, but an extraordinary sense of direction and independence on field trips. Rarely will we find a child with autism who appears either consistently high-functioning or low-functioning across environments and tasks.

Researchers generally report the age and sex of participants in a study. They also identify any other statistics considered important to the research project. Articles on autism often show subjects grouped according to language ability, I.Q., and known medical characteristics. Scholars don't all use the same categories to group their subjects. Some use an intelligence score or a specific skill level to divide their subjects into two subgroups. In another study the researcher may use a similar measurement, but divide the groups according to a different I.Q. score.

Another approach to subtypes has been offered by a researcher at Stanford University Medical Center. Dr. Bryna Siegel suggests that there are four behavioral subgroups ("Empirically Derived Subclassification of the Autistic Syndrome," *Journal of Autism and Developmental Disorders*, 1986). She looks at clusters of behavior, which she calls co-occurring because they appear at the same developmental stage. Dr. Siegel lists these types of autism:

1) Echolalic autism: Children repeat, or "echo," language, have poor language skills, and have a lot of stereotypic motor movements (hand-flapping, hopping, blinking) when excited.
2) Primitive autism: Children have profound mental retardation, little or no language, and a lot of continuous stereotypes (rocking, nodding, swinging)
3) Residual state autism: Similar to Asperger's syndrome; these individuals are odd, but not so withdrawn that they seem antisocial or unresponsive.
4) Negativistic autism: Children actively resist social contact, will push away or run away rather than act passive or ignore others.

This listing of subtypes represents a worthy effort of a very well-informed expert on autism. However, it doesn't have the advantage of clear and specific boundaries for each classification. A child may seem to move from one category to another and back again as he grows older. Furthermore, these four subgroups don't explain the remarkable number of different developmental patterns in autism.

It's neither helpful nor necessarily accurate to call a person with autism severely retarded. The latest research shows that some of the persons considered severely retarded just have neuromotor problems that keep them from responding to test instructions. A thorough evaluation should measure all of the person's abilities; this means their motor, verbal, and social skills as well as performance on intelligence tests. Some of the most challenging and unusual developmental patterns show up when we compare an individual's understanding with her or his expression. Chapter 11 will discuss this in greater detail.

We know that persons with autism, like people with stroke disorders, usually have different levels of fluency in the written or the spoken forms of language. One person might read well and fail to comprehend a conversation, while another understands what he hears, but can't recognize a word on a page. Some can speak or write, do neither, or both. The number of communication subtypes boggles our mind! We haven't found reliable ways of recognizing these subtypes yet.

Hopefully, researchers will pay more attention to learning styles rather than behavior in the future. Neurologists may discover the important subtypes, the different ways that information passes from one part of the brain to another.

We can't see the microscopic differences between peoples' neuromotor patterns, but we believe they are the reasons behind the different developmental problems. Those differences matter more than whatever behaviors we happen to notice and use to classify subgroups today.

Are there benefits to subclassifying autism?

Though we don't have an effective system for subclassifying people with autism yet, specialists have noticed different patterns of development. Knowing how similar students have responded to a particular activity will help teachers choose lesson plans for a new student.

Experienced teachers know the value of working with several students. Their exposure to many learning styles helps them see past the label of *autism* to focus on the individual student and her resemblance to others. In the absence of a reliable classification system, the best teachers have to rely on their personal encounters. However, commonly recognized subtypes would make it easier for teachers to share information between schools and research centers. Looking beyond medical subtypes to the differences in learning styles will help us choose the most effective teaching techniques for an individual with autism.

Researchers in various medical centers are already exploring the ways that people see, hear, and process information. Exciting revelations about the differences between human beings have already appeared. Some studies report that people with autism often have a different response to sights and sounds than the typical person. There's no common pattern within autism. Some people will experience distortion in only one sensory area, while others will have problems in several, perhaps even all.

Our next step is to explore the different patterns that make one person with autism so different from another. When we understand this, we will be able to shape our messages to the individual's learning style.

Do the different subtypes really have anything in common?

Though this chapter has focused mainly on the need to look at different forms of autism, it's still important to recognize the common characteristics of people with this diagnosis.

With the exception of Rett syndrome, which is no longer included as part of the autistic spectrum, all forms of this disability share these important features:

A) They are lifelong disabilities affecting communication and social skills.
B) They are caused by neurological differences, probably present from early fetal development.
C) They show up as highly individual responses to some or all of the five senses.
D) Individuals show uneven development in different skill areas, sometimes combining both extreme weaknesses and exceptional abilities.

Is there any point in using a single term, *autism*, to cover so many different patterns of the disability?

Unfortunately, medical terms tend to become frozen in bureaucratic or legal codes that resist change, in spite of new scientific information. For example, it took years to convince insurance companies, school districts, and other agencies that autism wasn't an emotional disorder, or a form of mental illness, as believed in the forties and fifties. Parent leaders thought they'd won a major victory when they got government regulations to include autism in the category of developmental disabilities. However, that proved to be only the first of many bureaucratic battles for people with autism.

When the "education for all" bill passed into law twenty years ago, it specifically mentioned the better-known disabilities such as mental retardation, hearing impairment, and vision impairment. It did not mention autism, so most state and local officials counted students with autism within the catchall category of "other health-impaired," an overly broad term that included children with kidney failure, hemophilia, and AIDS. Simply put, excluding autism from the language of the law meant that schools could ignore autism, assigning those students to teachers who had no specific training in that disability.

In 1990, the Autism Society of America succeeded in

amending the language of Public Law 101-476 to name autism along with the other specific learning disabilities. They hoped that the newly worded law would encourage schools to hire specially trained personnel and recognize that students with autism had needs that often weren't met in programs designed for those with mental retardation.

It took so long to write autism into law that many parents are afraid to see that term suddenly abandoned and replaced with new language. It could take another generation of lobbying to get federal and state regulations to recognize any newly named subtypes. Besides, most people with autism need similar services, in spite of their different learning patterns. So it seems practical to include them under one diagnostic term.

Some advocates argue that autism shouldn't be confused with similar disorders, such as Asperger's syndrome and pervasive developmental delay (PDD). They claim there is a boundary line between these terms, but others argue that the distinction is hypothetical, like the difference between a glass that is half full and one that is half empty. The truth is, we don't have clear evidence that would prove a particular individual belongs on one side or the other of many of these definitions' boundaries.

Medical syndromes often affect individuals differently. Not everyone with autism shows a standard, or "classic," set of symptoms, but the diagnosis has practical value. It offers a starting point for people who want to understand the individual's problems. As administrators have often observed, "It's taken all this time to recognize that there's something called autism. Why change the label now and spend another twenty years teaching a new term?" At this time, we don't have enough scientific evidence to abandon a fifty-year-old diagnosis in favor of a new set of labels.

REVIEW

At one time we had no way to recognize the differences between peoples' thought patterns, nor did we understand the neurological mechanism that sends signals from one part of the brain to another. Modern technology, however, has allowed us to discover and define some of the neurological differences behind autism.

The more we study these differences, the more we realize that autism is not a single disability that affects everyone the same way. Some people who used to be called autistic have been reclassified with a more specific medical diagnosis such as Rett syndrome. To date, only one form of autism, fragile X, can be diagnosed with a laboratory test. Further research will probably show us more subtypes in the future.

Discoveries of subtypes will improve our understanding of learning differences. Eventually, this should lead to better services. For the time being, the term *autism* still identifies a broad variety of people who, in spite of their differences, have many developmental problems in common.

What else should I read?

Cohen, Donald, Donnellan, Anne, and Paul., R., eds. *Handbook of Autism and Pervasive Developmental Disorders*. New York: Wiley, 1987.

For information on Fragile-X contact:

National Fragile X Foundation
1441 York Street, Suite 215
Denver, CO 80206
Phone: (303) 333-6155

For information on Rett syndrome, contact:

International Rett Syndrome Association
8511 Rose Marie Drive
Fort Washington, MD 20744
Phone: (301) 248-7031

5

Is It Hard to Tell If Someone Has Autism?

We look forward to the day when early diagnosis may be possible with a simple test, perhaps of genetic material such as chromosomes. Brain scans already offer potential for research, but we need more experience with this technology before using it as a diagnostic tool.

Parents often complain that it takes too long for their child with autism to receive an accurate diagnosis. First, months, or even years, pass before the mother realizes her child is unusual. Then, when she finally begins asking doctors for advice, their opinions often disagree. The search for an explanation or diagnosis can take several more years.

Few doctors will mention the term *autism* until they have ruled out every other possibility. For example, most children with autism don't answer questions or follow instructions well, so doctors usually ask for an ear examination to test for hearing problems first. Next, they may request a psychiatric evaluation or interview with a social worker.

More often than not, doctors will send the parents to specialists for second or third opinions. Along the way, parents often hear more than one diagnosis, that their child is "brain damaged," "atypical," or has a "pervasive developmental delay (PDD)."

Why does it take so long to get a diagnosis?

It's not easy to recognize a developmental disability in early childhood, especially if the child is so young that other children that age haven't developed speech or reasoning ability yet. Before a certain age, no child will have speech or reasoning ability, so it takes time before the deficits of autism become apparent. Sometimes even the best authorities on autism will say "wait and see."

As Chapter 4 explained, there are no simple blood tests or other physical markers that indicate a child has autism. The neurological differences won't show up without brain scans. Researchers won't use this technology on young children, because there's a potential risk in the use of radioactive material. It's also expensive and not considered reliable for general diagnosis at this time.

Like other developmental disorders, autism can't be diagnosed in a single observation. We have to observe the child's development, the changes, over time. The youngster may take years to show an unusual developmental pattern, one that the doctors will recognize and give a name to.

Autism has many symptoms that can seem either mild or serious, making diagnosis difficult for a doctor who has limited experience of the disability. Many professionals have never seen a person with autism until that first mother brings in a three-year-old with mysterious signs.

Often, doctors are reluctant to offer a diagnosis of autism. They may wonder, "Should I tell that mother that her child has autism? What if I'm wrong? Would the parents panic, get depressed, or give up hope?" These fears cross the minds of many doctors, for they know the public has an unrealistic view of autism as tragic and hopeless.

Faced with this dilemma, many professionals won't use

the label. Right or wrong, they fear that the diagnosis of autism would discourage the family and harm a child who needs extra attention and deserves every opportunity to succeed. When doctors think the label might hurt the child, they often hedge, writing another term, like PDD in the medical record.

Misunderstandings about autism frighten parents more than the truth. Still, many of the old, disproven beliefs and stereotypes continue to appear in print. In *Son-Rise*, Barry Kaufman shares his first impression of autism, calling it, "the most irreversible category of the profoundly disturbed and psychotic." No wonder he panicked when he noticed symptoms in his son! But people with autism are neither psychotic, nor necessarily profoundly disabled.

Kaufman's journey from despair to hope and positive action makes a powerful story. Against professional advice, he and his wife followed their own instincts. They diagnosed their son at the age of seventeen months. This diagnosis was subsequently confirmed by professionals although doctors advised them it was too early to begin treatment. However, the parents' early diagnosis of autism didn't discourage them, it motivated them.

How can we tell if a child has autism?

Most children with autism show delay in some of the common developmental milestones, especially in speech and socialization. Those with severe neuromotor problems may not speak at all; some babble repetitively; and another group speaks normally until around eighteen months, when they regress.

Children with the most profound social disorders may appear unable to recognize their own mothers during infancy. They may not pay attention to anyone, or play with other children. Some will also lag behind the typical child in motor skills, such as hand movements, posture, crawling, and walking. Remember, however, that these delays don't necessarily indicate autism; they could suggest another developmental disability.

The surest sign of autism is the child's attention. Does he seem interested in the things other children his age notice? Does she like the toys that other children her age play with? Or does the child seem uninterested in the things you would expect him to like?

When an infant or toddler seems tuned to a different channel, ignoring the sights and sounds that entertain others her age, it's a warning sign. If the child always prefers household objects to age-appropriate toys, or shows other unusual interests, he may have a different perspective than others his age. That difference may signal autism, another way of organizing information in a mind with unusual neurological patterns.

The neurological differences of a child can trigger many symptoms. For example, a child who is tactile defensive (overly sensitive to touch) may give early signals, trying to escape his mother's touch instead of cuddling. Another child might have a different threshold of hearing, or unusual reactions to sights, smells, or tastes. Problems sleeping or eating may mean the child doesn't understand the family's schedule.

No specific behavior proves a child has autism. And just as speech varies widely, children with autism can show any level of ability, from genius to severely disabled, in other areas. But a collection of differences can tip the scales. Children with autism seem generally out of touch or out of step with others their age. They may notice things that astound you. Their skills may amaze you. But they are hard to teach, because their attention seems focused on the wrong things.

If you know a child like this, you may have already taken the first step toward the diagnosis. Do that child a favor: suggest that the family take the next step, a discussion with their doctor. When parents notice that their child is constantly marching to a different drummer, it's time to ask for a professional evaluation.

Is it harder to diagnose autism in an adult?

From a bureaucratic perspective, it's harder to diagnose autism in an adult. Federal law says a developmental disability must begin before the age of twenty-one. If a person went undiagnosed throughout childhood, family members and teachers have to document that the person was, in fact, disabled before the age of twenty-one. The medical profession recognizes that autism is a neurological disorder, present from birth, that slowly becomes apparent in childhood. Accordingly, developmental history is important.

Some authorities argue that you cannot diagnose autism in an adult without having their childhood records. A family history, an interview with the parents, school records, or the baby book may prove the case. Without a developmental history, it's hard to tell the difference between an adult with autism and one who has suffered later forms of brain injury.

Like the rest of us, people with autism develop individuality, showing more differences in adult life than in childhood. We all seem pretty much alike for the first few years of life. Our later experiences—schooling, contact with parents and friends, etc.—have a great effect on our personality and behavior. By the age of twenty, thirty, forty, or fifty, personal history and environment have left their mark on all of us.

People with autism are affected by their environment as much as we are, but not necessarily in the way we would like. When people are treated as "different" and denied chances for personal choice, it often damages their self-esteem. Children with autism often need extra time to choose a cookie or pick a shirt from the closet, so others make the choices for them. It's often easier to do things for these children than to teach them to do things for themselves. However, this makes some children quit trying, leading them into a pattern of dependency.

Some of the old beliefs—that people with autism don't feel emotion, or can't love—need reexamination. Those assumptions were based on Kanner's first subjects, fifty years ago. None of those people had the opportunities we offer children today. They had no right to public education, no communication therapy, less chance for self-confidence. Their rejection and social isolation had taken a toll, adding to the problems of neurological disorder. No wonder doctors called them "withdrawn," "depressed," and "antisocial"!

More adults with autism are living and working in the community than ever before. Some even have college degrees. Yet many of the best educated still qualify for federal financial support because they can't manage their lives without some ongoing supervision. Often, they stay with their parents because they can't cope with the decisions of household management.

Who can diagnose autism?

Officially, only a physician or licensed psychologist can diagnose autism for the purposes of school placement, medical records, or eligibility for financial assistance or medical coupons. Such a diagnosis will usually hold up legally until challenged by another professional during reevaluation of a student or a dependent.

In reality, many teachers, preschool supervisors, and, yes, even parents, detect autism before a formal diagnosis. Experienced caregivers often spot the pattern before the doctor, who sees the child for only thirty minutes, twice a year. However, it takes an examination by an expert to give a thorough evaluation and diagnosis.

Since 1943, when Dr. Kanner prepared his checklist, authorities have developed better tools to recognize autism and measure its effects. There are numerous specialized tests, like CARS (Childhood Autism Rating Scale), that professionals may order to decide if an individual fits within the definition of autism. But these tests can be difficult to apply and evaluate unless the testor has experience and training in their use. Most psychologists won't attempt to administer CARS, but refer the parents to a specialist.

Many family doctors and pediatricians send the parents to a specialist to make the final evaluation. Most medical schools operate a developmental program that can diagnose autism and other severe learning disabilities.

Why do professionals often disagree?

Doctors, teachers, and psychologists generally have very little experience with autism unless their professional training specialized in developmental disabilities. Some have no more information than the parents, except for a textbook or clinical dictionary.

Since there are no physical signs of autism, no surefire tests to answer "yes" or "no," the diagnosis depends on a lot of "maybes." All of the developmental characteristics— speech, social behaviors, and sensory reactions—can vary tremendously from one youngster to another. It's hard for an examiner to judge whether a particular child has enough symptoms to indicate autism or is merely a child with a few unusual quirks. Ultimately, the diagnosis depends upon the skill of the professional and her or his personal judgment.

This can also be a painful responsibility for a professional—to look at a young child and realize that the notes entered into the medical chart may either open up or close off opportunities for that youngster's future. Knowing that many people assume the worst when they hear the word *autism*, some doctors won't use the term unless they consider the child severely disabled.

Sometimes, the doctor isn't aware of the full range of abilities included in the autistic spectrum. In many cases, the doctor won't diagnose autism, in the belief that another label will serve the child better, protecting him from the misunderstandings other people have about autism.

Whatever the reason behind the physician's thinking, parents are usually confused by the added delay in diagnosis, or the disagreements that go on between the various professionals who see their child.

Many parents consider it a relief when they finally get an honest diagnosis. Though they may have dreaded to hear that their child has autism, they're eager to understand their child and to make contact with families of similar children. Finally, the label provides a clue, directing the parents' attention to books and articles written on the subject of autism.

Many educators and parents think there's value in the diagnostic term *autism* because it identifies a type of learning disability. It also signals the need for certain kinds of services and entitlements.

Is there a difference between autism and pervasive developmental delay (PDD)?

This question confuses many people and the answer may confuse them even more. A very large number of people with autism, "within the autistic spectrum," or "affected by the syndrome of autism," will not be diagnosed with any of those terms. The more capable and verbal they are, the more likely their diagnosis will be called PDD (pervasive developmental delay), or, even more evasively, PDD-NOS (pervasive developmental delay, not otherwise specified).

What's going on? We are watching language change. When Dr. Leo Kanner described his first group of patients with his new-fangled label of *autism*, most of them had enough speech and self-help skills that they might be called high-functioning by a later generation of researchers. It was only after we discovered that some severely disabled people also had characteristics of autism that we began applying the term to people with such an incredible range of talents and abilities.

The "A-word" was supposed to help people, freeing them from a mistaken diagnosis like schizophrenia or mental retardation. But, as so often happens, the word became devalued through misuse. The most sensational, most severe cases of autism received the greatest publicity. The quiet, moderately disabled person (like Kanner's original patients) went unnoticed by journalists and television writers. Gradually, but surely, the public image of autism became like Barry Kaufman's first impression, that it was "the most irreversible category of the profoundly disturbed and psychotic."

Today, some professionals continue using the term *autism* as it was used thirty or forty years ago, to cover a very broad range of symptoms connected with language and social dysfunction. Others refuse to apply that diagnosis unless the individual shows extreme symptoms in every one of several areas. They call milder forms of the disability PDD.

Dr. Doris Allen, a developmental specialist at the Albert Einstein School of Medicine, calls PDD "a way of not diagnosing autism," a diagnosis doctors use when they want to avoid the word. PDD has become a professional euphemism, a soft term for something considered too harsh or too blunt.

People have the most well-intentioned reasons for avoiding the real diagnosis. They want to protect a child from a label that might trigger fear, rejection, and the loss of opportunities. I once heard a doctor confide to another, "I won't call this child autistic. That would be like throwing him on a trash heap where no one will ever give him a second chance."

That neurologist admits she will only diagnose autism in the most severe cases. Meaning well, she has become part of the problem. Every time doctors or psychologists refuse to call a more capable child autistic, they are narrowing the definition without scientific evidence. The diagnosis becomes more devalued, spiraling downward until there are fewer and fewer children with that diagnosis, and more and more diagnosed with PDD.

As long as we have no reliable biological tests to identify autism, it will be hard to qualify these people for services. Insurance companies, government regulations, and school services all rely on guidelines for eligibility and benefits. It took nearly forty years to convince officials that children with autism needed special education and communication therapy. All of those entitlements depend on the children having the keyword in their diagnosis. When they are called PDD or PDD-NOS, they can't get the benefits they need.

Reading this, you may well ask, What difference does the diagnosis make, anyway? Who cares? Good question! Labeling people just for the sake of categories makes no sense and can do a lot of harm. However, even the most capable people with autism need special education. Unfortunately, they can't get their entitlements if their diagnosis doesn't fit the language in the regulations.

We shouldn't ask medical authorities to rewrite scientific guidelines to fit political or economic policies. When researchers discover new subtypes or better ways to identify different forms of autism, let's rewrite the regulations for services. However, at this time, the arguments about autism and PDD have no scientific value. Public attitudes and the whim of the person conducting the diagnosis, not biological evidence, seem to determine who has autism and who has PDD.

Perhaps one day we'll offer people services based on their individual needs, not just their labels. Then, the diagnosis of autism, PDD, or Asperger's syndrome will no longer matter.

If the symptoms go away, does the person still have autism?

This question gets to the heart of a major disagreement between authorities. People who take one view say, "Autism is defined by behaviors; so if the autistic behaviors stop, the person no longer has autism." Some well-known writers have even told the world that their children are no longer autistic. One announced that this son's autism had been "cured," and that he was merely "retarded," a very modest success story. Others have boasted that a well-educated adult had "residual autism," or was a "recovered autistic."

Though we can't cure autism by changing a person's neurological pathways, education and training can work wonders for many people. It may look like "'curing," but the word *habilitation* describes the changes better. Chapter 13 will discuss approaches to education.

To habilitate simply means "to make able." A person with autism, like a person with any other disability, can often learn to succeed in many tasks. That doesn't mean the person no longer has autism. It means he or she has learned a new skill or overcome a disagreeable behavior.

When a person without sight uses braille scanners and typewriters, we don't say their blindness is "cured." We simply say the person has learned to function more like people with vision. We call it habilitation, not cure.

REVIEW

There are no biological tests that indicate autism in an infant. Symptoms only appear over time, as the child shows a pattern of developmental problems. Generally, children are two to three years old before they have enough symptoms for diagnosis.

Diagnosis is often delayed or incorrect because children with autism don't follow a single developmental pattern. These differences between individuals make diagnosis confusing for all but the most experienced professionals.

It's more difficult to diagnose autism in adults because they have been affected by years of environmental influences—education, health, and social life. Generally, the person's childhood records are used to support the diagnosis in adults.

Many teachers and parents are able to recognize the symptoms of autism and can then begin the quest for an official diagnosis. However, it takes an experienced specialist to do a professional evaluation. Often, professionals will disagree on the diagnosis because they have different definitions of autism.

Over the years, there has been a tendency for many professionals to avoid using the word *autism*, except in very severe cases. There are no accepted guidelines or biological tests to separate autism from PDD. Many people who would have been called autistic ten or twenty years ago are now diagnosed as having PDD.

Many people outgrow or overcome some of their autistic behaviors or symptoms. This probably doesn't signal a biological change, or mean they have overcome all of their neurological problems. It means they have matured and adapted, in spite of their condition.

What else should I read?

American Psychiatric Association. *Diagnostic and Statistical Manual of Mental Disorders*, Washington, D.C. American Psychiatric Association 1987 3rd ed., rev. (DSM-IIIR). This is the most commonly used reference for the definition of autism. Ironically, the definition has gone through revision in every one of the last three editions.

Cohen, D., Donnellan, A., and Paul, R., eds. *Handbook of Autism and Pervasive Developmental Disorders*. New York: Wiley, 1987.

Gillian, James E., ed. *Autism: Diagnosis, Instruction, Management, and Research*. Springfield, IL: C.C. Thomas, 1981.

Schopler, E., and Mesibov, G.B., eds. *Diagnosis and Assessment in Autism*. New York: Plenum, 1988.

6

Is There a Cure for Autism?

A number of parents have written about the "miracles" of their child's development. Often, these miracles merely mean that the parents had mistaken notions about autism before their child's successful habilitation.

Some of you will read this chapter first. Many parents skip past all of the information about diagnosis and symptoms to get right to it. Is there a cure? you may ask, and Who will cure my child?

If you are one of those impatient readers, if you ignored the definitions of autism and its many characteristics, this chapter may disappoint you.

In the medical sense, there is no cure for neurological disorganization. Not now, nor in the predictable future. Some problems, such as overactivity or obsessive–compulsive disorders, may respond to medication. But medical science offers few solutions for many of the problems of autism.

Parents have traveled around the world searching for a better treatment. Some have gone into debt, put their faith in religion, mystical treatments, and medical hoaxes. Even educated people have taken chances with strange and unproven therapies. Parents will try anything they think might help their child.

Though doctors say there is no such thing as a cure, stories of "miracles" show up in magazines almost every year. Parents wonder, "Who can I believe? Is there anything, short of a miracle, that will help my child?"

Is there any hope?

Absolutely! Parents and teachers can now do more for a child with autism than ever before, and the future seems even more promising. Adults, as well as children, are succeeding in ways we would have called impossible in the past.

Our understanding of autism has changed significantly since 1943, and the earlier searches for "cures" now seem unrealistic in terms of today's understanding of neurological problems. One major step comes with the recognition that physical healing or curing isn't the only way to help a person. People who are blind, deaf, or physically disabled don't need cures to enjoy life. They use braille, sign language, or physical supports to improve their lives.

We're finding better ways to help people cope with autism too. Not by changing the person's biology, but by changing part of the environment or our expectations for the individual.

Treatments have always been based on the professional's view of autism, right or wrong. When doctors believed autism was an emotional problem, they offered an emotional treatment, psychoanalysis. The parents, as well as the child, had to go through analysis to explain away the autism. This never worked, but books were published, clinics opened, and schools begun, all centered around this notion.

Some people still try therapies based on theories of autism that point to emotional causes. For example, "holding therapy" claims to heal the parent/child relationship. The mother is trained to give "therapy," holding her child until they have a bonding experience.

Today, few professionals believe in holding therapy or

other treatments based on emotion-related theories of autism. However, every year thousands of relatives, friends, or caring neighbors will read one of the older books and follow the mistakes of the past. They will pass the information along to parents and teachers who are eager to try anything.

In 1964, Dr. Bernard Rimland, a psychologist and father of a son with autism, wrote a world-renowned book, *Infantile Autism*. Dr. Rimland appealed to other professionals and parents to recognize that the psychoanalytic treatments had no benefit, that autism had to be understood and treated from another point of view.

After rejecting the emotional theory of autism, doctors searched for other explanations. For a while, many hoped to find a chemical irregularity, as had been found in mental illnesses such as schizophrenia and bipolar disorders. Some thought that diet, vitamins, or drugs would correct the problems of autism.

In the early 1980s a drug called fenfluramine seemed promising. A leading researcher, Dr. Edward Ritvo, discovered high levels of serotonin (a neurotransmitter, a chemical responsible for passing nerve impulses within the brain and nervous system) in some patients with autism. He thought those extra neurotransmitters might cause the autism, so he searched for a drug to lower the serotonin level.

Fenfluramine had been developed for diet control. And, as with most drugs, there were side effects. It lowered serotonin levels in the spinal fluid, so the doctor tried the drug as a treatment for autism. In the first experiment with four children, three seemed to improve. This premature news was rapidly blown out of proportion and newspapers reported a "cure" for autism.

Follow-up studies proved disappointing. While some people seemed to have better self-control with fenfluramine, they soon grew accustomed to the drug and had to go off medication from time to time in order to benefit again.

The follow-up studies had another surprise: serotonin levels didn't predict the drug's effect, calling into question the whole justification for using it to lower serotonin levels. Some people with high serotonin levels didn't benefit at all, while some with normal biochemistry did!

New discoveries have shown us that we must consider other factors in autism besides brain chemistry. Electronic brain scans and autopsies have revealed differences in brain shape and structure. Medicine can't change those. That's the bad news. But there's good news too.

Thanks to neurological research, we now understand the mind and its circuitry better than we did a few years ago. The science of neuroanatomy is exploring the links between brain structure, learning, and behavior. What we can't change, we may learn to use more efficiently.

Today, habilitation is our best hope of treating autism, helping people function in spite of their neurological differences. We can't change those yet. But people with autism can overcome many of the symptomatic behaviors that used to cause problems for so many.

What is the difference between *cure* and *habilitation*?

To cure means "to restore to health, soundness, or normality." To habilitate means "to qualify, or make more able." Both promise help, but through different paths.

There's no "restoring to normality" in autism, because there was never a *normality* to restore. The disability began before birth, during the growth of brain cells. But habilitation can teach a person to function in spite of the challenges brought on by the disability.

It's hard to imagine coping with a condition like autism, because we can't "see" the person's barriers to life. There are no outward clues as to which brain cells or neurological pathways are impaired, making speech or reasoning difficult. It's easier to understand someone whose problems are connected to a specific and visible organ, like loss of hearing from a problem in the ear or lack of sight due to damage to the eyes.

Imagine losing your sight. Turn out the lights or cover your eyes. After your first panic, you will start to understand the world of the sightless. You no longer get signals from color, light, or moving objects. Your loss of vision has an obvious effect on your reaction to the environment.

Without sight, you behave differently. You bump into things. You don't recognize people unless you hear their voices or touch them. You don't read. You have "symptoms of blindness." By turning the lights back on you can "cure" all those symptoms: you read again, recognize others by their appearance, and move around obstacles.

If you had no miracle switch to restore your sight, if you lost your vision permanently, you'd need to adjust to life without the sense of sight. We can help people do this, and we can help people cope with autism through habilitation, too.

Habilitation teaches people to adapt, substituting a strength for a weakness. Those who can't process information through one sense may try another. Braille substitutes touch for sight. Sign language uses gesture and vision in place of sound and hearing.

Equipment such as communication boards, charts, or pictures help many people with autism, just as others use hearing aids, wheelchairs, and Seeing Eye dogs. When we recognize an individual's challenge, we can adjust our expectation and help the person succeed in his or her own way. Computer technology has untapped potential for habilitating people with disabilities like autism. We'll explore this more deeply in Chapter 12.

Why are there so many stories about "miracles"?

True miracles are supposed to be answered prayers, supernatural solutions to human concerns. But there's another way to define miracles, that is, as events that can't be explained through our present understanding of nature. Simply stated, the less people knew about autism, or understood habilitation, the more miraculous a successful therapy appeared.

In our ignorance twenty or thirty years ago, we considered autism a hopeless mental disorder. Any progress made by a person with autism seemed miraculous during that unenlightened period. However, we know more about autism today and have seen many people develop in ways that once would have been called miraculous. Several have been the subject of books.

In *Emergence: Labeled Autistic*, Temple Grandin tells how she learned to control her symptoms, start a successful career, and earn a Ph.D. Her autobiography proves that a genius with autism can learn to cope with her disability. The book has no formula to guarantee everyone the same success. Temple, like Helen Keller, may be one of a kind, a pioneer with remarkable intelligence that let her overcome the challenge of her disability.

On the other hand, some stories about miracles turn out to be more disappointing. In some cases, we find that the "miracle" was simply based on a misunderstanding. Perhaps the diagnosis had been wrong, or the parents had an inaccurate set of expectations. For example, the child in Mary Callahan's *Fighting for Tony* never had autism. He had been misdiagnosed by doctors who had limited understanding of developmental disabilities. The "miracle" happened when Tony's mother read about cerebral allergies and discovered her son's violent and uncontrollable behaviors resulted from an extremely rare form of milk allergy.

When Barry Kaufman developed imitation therapy for his son, he thought it was a cure. In the book, *Son-Rise*, he explains that he and his wife rejected therapies based on punishment and compliance training, so they invented their own, hoping to motivate the child to come out of his shell.

"We knew that if we could get Raun to want to participate with us," Kaufman wrote, "he would then make the new connections, open new channels. He could do it or at least he would try, not by simple training or rote memory, not by conditioning, but by the energy and internal efforts that would come as the fruits of his own desire."

Kaufman believed that he could motivate his son to heal himself, making new neurological connections. He likened this process to the rehabilitation of some stroke patients. Biological research doesn't support this theory, although neurologists now believe early intervention provides stimulation to a child's developing cerebellum.

Should you believe in miracles?

Most of the books published on autism have been sincere. The writers believed what they wrote. We shouldn't blame them for the mistakes of their time, misunderstandings they shared with the best authorities of the day. The Kaufmans claimed that twelve hours of imitation therapy a day can motivate a child to break through the barriers of autism. This approach hasn't produced miracles for the families who try the Kaufmans' method or attend their Options Institute. However, many of these parents and children seem happier after the experience. They may also have better interactions, but a cure has nothing to do with it.

The "miracle" in Kaufman's second book, *A Miracle to Believe In*, is emotional, not neurological. Kaufman himself explains, *"If the rebirth of a child and the rebirth of those who loved, accepted, and worked with him is called a miracle . . . then miracles will happen only to those who believe in them."*

In an interview for the Autism Society of America's newsletter, Mary Callahan offered other parents this advice: *"You're entitled to your hope. But you are also justified to give up hope when you encounter a dead end. Perhaps you will find hope again when new information becomes available. Remember, there are many kinds of success. Not every parent's success will mean a complete recovery. There are smaller successes too, and parents should feel accomplishment in reaching those."*

What if a symptom goes away? Does it mean there's been a cure?

People still argue about this question. Some say changes in appearance or behavior are only cosmetic, making a person with autism *look* more like others. They point out that neurological differences still hide beneath the "normal" gestures the person has learned. The individual still has autism and the carefully repressed symptoms will be obvious in times of stress or in unfamiliar settings.

Others call autism a behavioral pattern. They say that getting rid of the "autistic behaviors" erases the autism. Fewer people hold this view today than in the seventies and early eighties. At that time, there wasn't much neurological evidence to explain autism. Some of the best authorities thought they could cure autism by changing or modifying the behavior.

Some teachers and psychologists still boast that their treatment makes students "apparently normal." These trainers identify behaviors considered symptomatic of autism (hand-flapping, walking on the toes, or self-stimulation) and work out a plan to stop those behaviors. They also select a group of gestures that represent "normal" social behavior and train the student to perform on command.

After months, or even years, of hearing a trainer command, "Look at me!" most students develop the habit of looking speakers in the eye. Some will learn to look a stranger in the eye, offer a firm handshake, and repeat a greeting such as "Nice to meet you," or "You can call me Pete."

It's impressive to see how normal some of these graduates appear in a first contact, but this impression fades when conversation drifts into new or unfamiliar areas. Generally, there's no real habilitation behind these well-learned social gestures. The student now looks people in the eye, but he probably still misses the subtle clues that the rest of us seek from eye contact. We must ask, Has the child *learned* to appear normal, or has the therapist only trained the child to *imitate* a behavior that's still unnatural to her or him?

Cynics compare this type of therapy to animal training. When a circus performer trains a horse to "count" by stamping its hoof a certain number of times, the horse hasn't really understood the concept of numbers, let alone the language of the trainer. Rather, the horse has learned to perform a totally unnatural behavior on cue. The only functional value to the horse is the reward after the performance. Some therapists for students with autism also depend heavily on M&M's or similar rewards. They motivate the student with candy because the tasks themselves have no motivating or functional value to the learner.

Ivar Lovaas, a psychologist at UCLA, pioneered the technique of "behavior modification" for people with autism. In a highly controlled environment, Lovaas and his followers used rewards and punishments to train students to copy the behaviors of typical children. Many teachers still follow Lovaas's philosophy, using the term *compliance training* when forcing a student to comply with the teacher's orders and *operant conditioning* when planning a system of rewards and punishments.

During his early research, Lovaas experimented with techniques no longer accepted in his profession. In *A Child Called Noah*, Josh Greenfield tells about his family's journey to Los Angeles in the hope that the famous Lovaas program at UCLA would help his son, Noah.

Greenfield watches his child go through the steps of compliance training as the teachers teach discipline: "If most of the operant conditioning is nothing less than old-fashioned dog training, it is something I don't scoff at. I must admit, though, that on the rare occasions Noah is struck during a treatment, I flinch and clench my fists. . . . But then I remind myself that what love and affection can't always accomplish, perhaps fear and duress can."

"These kids don't have any fear at all." Lovaas explained. "And to begin to make them function, you must forget any etiology [*cause of the disorder*] and implant fear in them. . . . If Noah was afraid of an electric shock, I'd use my stinger on him tomorrow." He eventually recommended a thirty-six hour fast, to see if he could make food a more powerful motivator for the child. The fast only made the boy violently ill.

Progress in civil rights and standards for treating psychological subjects has changed some of Lovaas's methods, but the philosophy of this treatment remains the same. It is, in essence, to use rewards and punishments to make the child behave according to our social standards.

The theory and outcome, however, hasn't changed since 1970. "I promise no miracles . . ." Lovaas told Greenfield. "A lot will depend on the ability of you and your wife to learn the therapies. Because, if the treatments are not kept up, no matter what advances your boy makes, he will eventually backslide." In other words, once the therapists get results from certain rewards and punishments, the parents must continue the same techniques forever.

This method sometimes changes the behavior or appearance of the child. However, it doesn't prepare the person to cope with new situations, especially circumstances that don't provide the punishment/reward conditions familiar to the child. The apparent cure turns out to be a cure in appearance only.

There's another force behind behavior change, the biological calendar. As Chapter 1: ("What Is Autism?") explains, this is a developmental disability. The symptoms show up as delays or disturbances in the development of the child. A symptom can be either an odd behavior, skills appearing out of order, or lags in the child's ability to reach typical childhood milestones. Any or all of these difficulties may change as the person grows or develops into adulthood.

Every parent who has written about autism complains

about the developmental mysteries of this disability. They simply cannot predict the child's future—how long a problem will persist or what changes another year might bring.

Remember, *a symptom of autism is not autism itself.* The symptom merely offers a clue that the individual is somehow different from the average. That difference is not just behavioral, it is neurological.

The neurological challenge can outlast a particular behavior such as hand-flapping, walking on tiptoe, and certain language difficulties. Even symptoms such as seizure disorders may wane or disappear as the person grows older. Other symptoms may change with age, growth, or habilitation. As you watch a person with autism go through changes of behavior, ask yourself: *"Was the behavior outgrown? Was it replaced by another behavior? Is the person responding to operant conditioning in a certain environment? Will this behavior show up in another setting, or has real change occurred?"*

Can you tell if a particular treatment will help an individual?

Many treatments—drugs, habilitation plans, and other therapies—offer limited help to some individuals. Parents often ask, *"Will it help my child? Is it worth the effort? How can I tell if my child will benefit?"*

These are good questions. Few people have the time or money to try every treatment that has boasted success for only a few people with autism. Besides, there are dangers in trying every approach that has been used.

The person with autism, like all other people, is an individual first, a person with a disability second. Changing diet, giving drugs, or switching training programs too often can confuse this person, creating problems as great as the original neurological problem.

The following chapters explore many treatments for autism.

However, a common warning applies to all of them: **Make sure the treatment matches the needs of the individual.**

News stories often report treatments for autism but leave out information about the particular individuals treated or the problems they had before treatment. Parents are easily confused by these reports of "cures." In reality, the treatment usually applies to specific problems experienced by a small number of people. Another person with autism who has different neurological or biological problems might be harmed by the same treatment.

Sensory disturbances, such as overreaction or underreaction to touch, raise important considerations when choosing a treatment. Treatments suitable for a child with a low pain threshold will be uncomfortable or disturbing to a child who is already too sensitive.

Professional journals generally tell the reader more about the people who tried a drug or therapy, their problems, and their response to the treatment. Doctors and teachers who understand the many characteristics of autism can help parents sort through the different types of treatment.

The basic questions to keep in mind include:

A) *What are the goals of a particular treatment? What biological and/or behavioral problems does this concern?*

B) *What are the problems of my child? Is there a match between my child and those who seem to benefit from this treatment?*

REVIEW

The search for a cure has changed during the last fifty years. Technology and research have taught us more about the neurological basis of autism. Today, we no longer expect to find cures through psychotherapies or medication alone.

The current focus of treatment is habilitation, helping the

individual function in spite of disabilities that can't be totally overcome.

Autism is not hopeless, nor necessarily tragic. People with this condition can become less dependent and lead happier lives than we once believed. A number of parents have written about the "miracles" of their child's development. Often, these miracles merely mean that the parents had mistaken notions about autism before their child's successful habilitation.

Some psychologists have claimed that autism is merely a set of behaviors, that changing the behaviors meant treating, even curing, the autism. Yet, behaviors often change during childhood, especially if there is a developmental disability. Effective education can help change behaviors, but that doesn't mean the underlying neurological challenge is gone. The person still has autism, in spite of behavioral change.

The many forms and degrees of autism make choosing a treatment difficult. Some techniques work well with some individuals, but not with others. Parents must decide whether a therapy matches their child's needs, or not.

What else should I read?

Callahan, Mary. *Fighting for Tony*. New York: Simon & Schuster, 1987.

Greenfield, Josh. *A Child Called Noah*. New York: Holt, Rinehart & Winston, 1971.

Kaufman, Barry. *A Miracle to Believe In*. Garden City, New York: Doubleday & Co., 1981.

———. *Son-Rise*. New York: Harper & Row, 1976.

Rimland, Bernard. *Infantile Autism: The Syndrome and Its Implications for a Neural Theory of Behavior*. New York: Appleton-Century-Crofts, 1964.

7

What Can Medication Do for People with Autism?

Drug therapy is not a substitute for other treatments, but should be part of a plan that includes opportunities for habilitation. Without educational therapies, drugs promise no long-lasting benefits.

How do medicines work?

Modern medicine can solve many health problems. The easiest to manage are those caused by contagious disease; vaccination can prevent the invasion of many forms of virus and antibiotics can counter an attack of bacteria.

Some health problems, like diabetes and hypertension, won't be permanently cured by a drug, but daily medication keeps the problem under control. This is also true for some forms of mental illness.

We know that schizophrenia and bipolar disorders are caused by an imbalance or disturbance of the brain's chemistry. Fluids called neurotransmitters regulate the nervous system. They carry or block signals from one part of the brain to another. When those neurotransmitters fail or become overactive, they create disturbances of thought, emotion, and behavior in a certain type of patient.

The right antipsychotic drug can help many people with mental illnesses function better. The chemical cure is part of the patient's overall treatment, similar to a diabetic's dependence on insulin to regulate the amount of insulin in the blood.

Yet, autism is not a mental illness. It is not caused merely by problems of brain chemistry or neurotransmitters. Therefore, antipsychotic drugs don't have the same effect on patients with autism as on patients with psychotic disorders.

It's true that some people with autism have unusual levels of neurotransmitters. But that doesn't seem to be the central cause of the disability. Research shows differences in brain structure, problems that won't go away with drug treatment or other "chemical cures" (See Chapter 3: "What Causes Autism?").

Why are drugs prescribed so often for autism?

There are many reasons for this. First of all, our society is very drug-dependent. Even healthy, nondisabled people take a variety of drugs to feel better, lose weight, stay awake, go to sleep, or treat everyday nuisance ailments like headaches.

Drugs seem to offer quick changes. We expect to see results as soon as a drug goes through the stomach lining and into the bloodstream. If there's going to be an effect, it starts to show up within days, hours, or even minutes. Other treatments, such as physical therapy or training, often take weeks or longer.

Parents can become desperate. A hyperactive child might sleep only a few minutes at a stretch. Others don't follow the family's time schedule. They may sleep during the day or wake up in the middle of the night, making normal routines impossible for the rest of the family. It's no wonder that parents will try treatments that offer quick changes in their child's behavior.

Unfortunately, drugs can have side effects we don't want to see. Sometimes these take years to show up. For this reason, the Food and Drug Administration acts slowly to approve new drugs, especially for use by young, still-developing children. Parents should act as cautiously as the FDA.

Don't rush to put your child on a new "miracle" drug. Serious physicians want to see studies that have tested a medication with a number of patients before they will prescribe it to their own. It may take a few months, possibly a year, before results are in. Rest assured that as soon as scientific evidence shows that a medicine offers more help than harm, the news travels fast through medical journals and parent organizations.

How does medication change behavior?

It doesn't. That's right. *Medicine doesn't change behavior!* Instead, a drug affects the biology of the body. If a behavior grows out of the body's chemistry and the drug changes that chemistry, the behavior may change as a result. That's a biological chain reaction, not a pill's direct signal to the brain that changes one, and only one, behavior.

If medicine could really change behavior, no one would be overweight, no one would have problems quitting smoking or overcoming substance abuse. We would all take drugs to improve our lives. If medicine could really change behavior, we would try "neat pills" and "polite pills" on typical children. But drugs don't deliver simple, desired behavior changes. At best, antipsychotic drugs slow down or speed up parts of the nervous system, regulating the activities which, in turn, cause what we call behavior.

No one should prescribe drugs to change behavior without understanding the reasons behind the behavior. However, doctors who know more about psychotic disorders than they do about developmental disabilities sometimes mistake patients with autism for those with a delusionary form of mental illness. They might assume that people with similar behaviors should have the same reaction to drugs, regardless of the individuals' different diagnoses. This simply doesn't work: antipsychotic drugs do not help people with autism.

A medicine that restores the delicate chemical balance in the brain for psychotic patients won't have the same effect on a patient with a developmental disability like autism. Unfortunately, if the first prescription doesn't work, sometimes the doctor may prescribe a larger dose. The side effects usually get worse. Enough medication eventually stops all behavior, including consciousness . . . and the breath of life.

Drugs also have other unintentional side effects. When a drug lowers anger or anxiety, it usually slows all other responses as well, including the ability to focus on sights or sounds, and physical coordination. If a drug stops an unwanted behavior, it may also stop a desirable activity. It may interfere with learning, social awareness, or even the drive for independence.

Which drugs are prescribed for autism?

Of course, a person with autism may need the same variety of cold pills, aspirin, and drugs for miscellaneous health problems as the rest of us. There's a difference between medicine for an individual and drug treatment for a disability. In other words, medicine taken for various health problems, including the control of a seizure disorder, isn't necessarily a treatment for the autism and can help maintain the physical health of a person.

The developmental problems that underly many symptoms of autism won't respond to chemical treatment. There simply are no drugs to correct deficits in language or reasoning ability. Autism can't be cured by any known group of drugs. However, some medications may be included in the treatment of certain symptoms of autism.

Dr. Magda Campbell, a renowned medical researcher at New York University, believes that some behavior problems may be reduced by appropriate drugs, but warns: "We do not believe drugs should be prescribed to control children's behaviors; we view drug treatment as part of a comprehensive treatment program. When an autistic child (or adult) displays symptoms which may be reduced by drug therapy, then the role of the drug is to make the person more amenable to other treatments, including special education and behavior therapy."

Campbell warns, "Special precautions are required when additional drug therapy is prescribed to autistic persons who suffer from associated seizure disorder and who are receiving antiseizure medication." Of equal concern, the physician must match the medication with the specific symptoms of the patient, since none of the various drugs address symptoms common to all people with the diagnosis of autism.

Four types of drugs are sometimes prescribed for behavior control of people with autism:

A) stimulants
B) antidepressants
C) opiate-antagonists
D) major tranquilizers

Each class of drugs works in a different manner.

A) *Stimulants,* such as Ritalin, are supposed to make a person more energetic and alert. They work for many people. For reasons we don't understand, they sometimes have the reverse effect on children who are already hyperactive. Sometimes these drugs make children calmer so they slow down and seem to concentrate longer. However, the drug may limit growth or have other negative side effects.

What Can Medication Do for People with Autism?

B) Antidepressants: Some antidepressants seem to help certain individuals with autism. We don't really understand the process, but Temple Grandin has written that her medication helps her focus, making it easier to cope with distractions. Other individuals seem to think more clearly and follow conversations better with the right antidepressant. There are very few risks or side effects from this type of medication, but changes may be so minor that they are hard to observe.

C) Opiate-antagonists counter the effects of natural opiates in the system. Many people, including those who get a "natural high" from long-distance running, produce endorphins that dull pain. The opiate-antagonists block the patient's reaction to either narcotics or the natural endorphins. This makes some individuals appear more responsive or attentive to their environment, and may increase tactile sensitivity.

For years researchers have known that some people with autism have abnormally low responses to pain. When the sensitivity to touch is dulled, a person misses a lot of physical feedback. Painful consequences (such as the hot stove top or bruised knuckles) become less important when the pain can't be felt.

Some violent or self-abusive people have naturally high levels of opiates in their system. These can block pain signals that might otherwise play a role in changing behaviors. The opiate-antagonists are often prescribed for alcoholics, drug addicts, and patients with high natural opiate levels.

The drug naltrexone has raised high hopes among some doctors and parents. The FDA hasn't approved naltrexone for treatment of autism yet. However, researchers believe it may benefit a certain type of patient, bringing the sense of touch within the normal range. It should make the person avoid painful behaviors and pay more attention to touch and therefore to social contact.

If follow-up studies on naltrexone support the claims, this drug may become an important part of the overall treatment for people with violent and abusive behavior. It may even encourage sociability. However, it may not affect a person's ability to speak or to reason. Furthermore, drugs of this type could backfire for a patient who is already too sensitive to touch. Opiate-antagonists might make touch more painful for a person who is already tactile defensive or overly sensitive to touch.

D) *Major tranquilizers*, including the antipsychotic or neuroleptic drugs, are often prescribed, but carry the greatest risks of unwanted side effects. Peter A. Breggin, M.D., offered this testimony (Pennsylvania House Select Committee on Autism, May 6, 1988):

These medications are not true "tranquilizers"; they do not produce a calm state of mind or a pleasant, relaxing experience such as some people associate with alcohol or the minor tranquilizers like Valium. Instead, they produce numbness or indifference. As doses increase, they cause apathy and lethargy, very similar to the mental fatigue that overcomes people with severe physical illness, such as the flu. Like sick people, the drug-treated patients withdraw from the world and show disinterest in their own well-being.

These drugs disrupt key neurological pathways involving frontal lobes, producing a "chemical lobotomy." Like surgically lobotomized patients, the drug-treated child shows less passion, imagination, curiosity and social involvement with others. Learning, maturation, and more complex adaptions to the world are impaired.

Every drug has an array of side effects, including some that may go undetected for years. For this reason, doctors generally begin a prescription with the lowest possible dose and are cautious about the medication. As a rule, physicians review the patient's response to treatment before continuing long-term use of any drug.

What are the risks of using these medications?

The neuroleptic drugs can do the most harm. They were never designed to treat specific problems of autism, but rather to control or eliminate behaviors of psychotic patients who may have delusions. Dr. Breggin warns:

> Along with numbness or indifference, the major tranquilizers or neuroleptics produce several painful and disabling neurological syndromes.
>
> One is Parkinsonism, which slows down all bodily movements and hobbles walking. Another is akathisia, which produces a very painful inner drive to keep in motion at all times.
>
> If we view the numbness as a chemical lobotomy, we may view some of the disabling neurological symptoms as a chemical straightjacket.
>
> These highly toxic major tranquilizers or neuroleptics produce myriad physical side effects and sometimes lethal reactions. But they cause one particular disease which is especially devastating. It is called tardive dyskinesia (late-developing motor disorder). After several months to several years of treatment with these agents, one-third to one-half or more patients will develop tardive dyskinesia. In some cases, the disease becomes permanent. There is no known treatment. . . . In adults, the first signs often appear around the face, mouth or tongue. Bizarre blinking, chewing, or tongue protrusions will disfigure the person and make him look "crazy". . . . Recent studies have begun to confirm that the drugs also produce a tardive (late-occurring) psychosis or drug-induced "craziness."

Dr. Breggin notes that the neuroleptics are most often abused in institutions. Patients living under the same roof can develop similar behaviors in spite of different biological problems. Sometimes the staff assumes that a particular drug will have the same effect on everyone. They often request drugs for patients who seem "unmanageable."

This creates pressure on the medical staff to try drugs as a solution to institutional behaviors. If a small amount doesn't change the patient's behavior, sometimes they raise the dosage. The patient may end up with a dangerously high level of a drug that offers no benefits, only the side effects—loss of energy, attention, and concentration.

Who should prescribe drugs?

Most physicians don't see many patients with autism and so it's hard for them to gain experience with the different drug treatments. Families may have to search far and wide for a doctor who understands the problems of autism and when and how to use drug therapy.

"Drug therapy should be prescribed only by physicians," Dr. Campbell warns. "Not all physicians, and not all psychiatrists or child psychiatrists have experience with psychoactive drugs. Certain child psychiatrists, pediatric neurologists or pediatricians are knowledgeable in this area. Perhaps the family physician, or the local county Medical Society should be consulted."

Always keep in mind that the purpose of prescription drugs is to help the patient, not to put the person in a "chemical straightjacket" for the convenience of others. Don't use medicine as a quick fix for behavior if that medication may also interfere with learning and development.

Sometimes nonmedical personnel will ask parents to medicate a child. A teacher may recommend a drug, even suggest a doctor who will prescribe something to make the child behave better in class. In extreme cases, schools want the parents to agree to drug treatment as part of the child's Individual Education Plan. This is not appropriate unless the child's own doctor agrees. A student has the right to attend school with a drug-free mind. The law guarantees this.

On the other hand, knowledgeable physicians may prescribe a medicine for long-term control of a biological problem or for short-term control of behavior during a specific crisis. Some individuals have cycles of temper or mood problems. These may occur only once a year or more often.

A doctor needs to review a patient's medical history to see if there is a pattern of biologically caused behavior problems. In some cases, the person needs a calming drug during these difficult periods. Still, a good comprehensive treatment plan should include measures to phase out the medication as quickly as possible.

How do drugs work as part of a *comprehensive treatment program?*

A comprehensive treatment program considers everything that affects a patient's overall health and welfare. It includes diet, exercise, and all of the other activities that affect the physical and emotional well-being of a person.

Dr. Campbell warns, "We do not believe that pharmacotherapy is indicated for 'behavior management' only." In other words, drug therapy is not a substitute for other treatments, but should be part of a plan that includes varied opportunities for habilitation. Without educational therapies, drugs promise no long-lasting benefits.

It's pointless to give students drugs just to make them manageable in school. Children don't learn by sitting quietly in a drug-induced stupor, and adults will never master vocational skills if they have to be heavily sedated for the ride to work. A "comprehensive treatment program" considers the trade-offs between therapies. It means looking for a variety of solutions, instead of always relying on medicine.

Sometimes a temporary drug treatment will help someone adjust to a new home, a different school, or a change of staff. Drugs might make the transition easier, but the prescription should include a plan for stopping the drug, not continuing it forever.

A comprehensive treatment plan doesn't use drugs to solve the *caretaker's* problems. Nor does it mean controlling every thought and action of the patient. We should use all resources—medicine, education, and family—to help the person function and foster a sense of well-being. When people with autism develop choice and expression, they have fewer behavior problems.

REVIEW

Medicines don't provide simple, permanent solutions for the problems associated with autism. They can't cure the problems of neurological disorders. However, drugs are often prescribed to reduce some of the challenging behaviors of people with autism.

Medications don't simply change behaviors, but they may affect biological problems, such as hyperactivity, that make an individual hard to teach and harder to live with. Four types of drugs—stimulants, antidepressants, opiate-antagonists, and heavy tranquilizers—are sometimes used to treat specific causes of behavior or learning problems.

The heavy tranquilizers, also called neuroleptics, have a number of dangerous, in some cases permanent, side effects. Overuse of these drugs may cause physical and mental symptoms that make the person even more disabled than before drug treatment began.

There is a critical shortage of doctors with experience in drug treatment for autism. Parents may have to contact their state medical society or a nearby medical school to find a doctor to trust with drug treatments.

Drugs can play an important role in the overall treatment of an individual. However, medication cannot take the place of good educational programs and other therapies.

What else should I read?

The *Journal of Autism and Developmental Disorders* and the *Journal of the American Academy of Child and Adolescent Psychiatry* often publish articles on medicines used to treat patients with autism.

The *Index Medicus* (found in all medical libraries) lists references for every article published on drugs. By looking up a drug by name, the reader will learn where to find more information.

Breggin, Peter R. *Psychiatric Drugs: Hazards to the Brain.* New York: Springer, 1983.

———. "On the Dangers of Medication for Institutionalized Children." *Advocate,* Vol. 21, No. 3, (1989).

Campbell, Magda. "Ask the Experts: *The Advocate* Interviews Dr. Magda Campbell." *Advocate,* Vol. 20, No. 4, (1988).

Coleman, Mary and Gillberg, Christopher. *Biology of the Autistic Syndrome.* New York: Praeger, 1987.

8

Do Special Diets Help?

Very few doctors think diet affects children with autism differently than other people. Research has never proven a connection between nutrition and this disability. However, many parents continue to look for a connection between their child's behavior and certain foods. Some think they have found one.

Medical treatments often disappoint parents. Either the drugs don't have any effect on autism, or they have side effects that interfere with learning. Besides, medicine requires a doctor's prescription. When drugs offer no help, parents who want to "try everything" often turn to treatments they can control themselves, such as the use of vitamin supplements and other diet changes.

As we saw in Chapter 3, diet *cannot* cause autism. Neither the diet of a pregnant mother, nor what her child eats after birth, creates the neurological problems or behaviors. Nevertheless, diet is a popular home treatment for everything from hyperactivity to drowsiness. No one needs a prescription to buy vitamins. Almost everyone, it sometimes seems, feels free to recommend them, be they grandparents, clerks in the health food store, or neighbors. Diet supplements seem like inexpensive, low-risk medicines.

Do Special Diets Help?

The boundary between nutrition and medicine isn't always clear. Food and drugs both contain chemical substances that may affect our physical and mental health in both positive and negative ways. We eat chemical compounds, either in their natural state (fresh or raw) or in some chemically altered form (cooked, preserved, or processed). The Food and Drug Administration tests all new drugs and food products before allowing them on the market. Research has to show that the substance is harmless, even when laboratory animals consume huge doses.

Almost anything we buy in a supermarket or health food store is "safe" to eat. We don't have to worry about the purity or safety of our foods so much as the balance in our diet. Our bodies need a variety of nutrients on a regular basis. Over time, a lack of any dietary essential can trigger a chain reaction, shutting down body functions and causing disease or even death.

Lack of niacin (one of the B vitamins) causes a nutritional disorder called pellagra. Pellagra has many symptoms: scaly and discolored skin, loss of texture on the tongue, diarrhea, and mental confusion. This last symptom can lead to psychosis or delirium. A person with pellagra may seem schizophrenic until treated nutritionally.

At one time, half the inmates at many insane asylums had pellagra-caused dementia. Once diagnosed, doctors could cure these people with a few cents' worth of niacin. Though this treatment worked only with nutritionally induced psychosis, some people hoped the same vitamin therapy would cure other forms of mental illness. They considered vitamin B to be "brain food."

In the 1960s Dr. Linus Pauling coined the term *orthomolecular therapy* to describe "the treatment of mental disease by the provision of the optimum molecular environment for the mind, especially the optimum concentration of substances normally present in the body."

In simpler language, Dr. Pauling recommended nutritional therapy for mental illness. He thought some people had a shortage of key chemicals in the brain: either nutrients were missing in the diet, or the system hadn't processed them properly. He suggested that a proper diet and large supplements of vitamins and minerals would cure such people.

Dr. Pauling was neither a physician nor a nutritionist, but, as a winner of two Nobel prizes (one for chemistry and one for peace) he had a worldwide reputation as scientist and statesman. His ideas attracted international attention twenty years ago. At that same time, physicians were experimenting with new antipsychotic drugs. For a while, it seemed that medicine and diet therapy were following the same path, toward a chemical cure. After decades of research, however, megavitamin research has not proven itself effective.

Do megavitamins help people with autism?

Later research on autism drew attention away from orthomolecular psychiatry. Autopsies of people who had lived with autism showed differences in brain structure. More and more research had the same findings: the important differences in autism were in brain *structure*, not in brain *chemistry!*

In the seventies, biochemistry revolutionized the treatment of schizophrenia, depression, and bipolar disorders. Some scientists hoped to find a "chemical cure" for developmental disabilities as well. One approach was that of Dr. William Hoffer, who coined the term *megavitamin therapy* to describe large doses of vitamins used to treat every mental disorder. Like Pauling, Hoffer believed the body could metabolize vitamins to produce chemicals needed for brain functioning.

Hoffer founded the *Journal of Orthomolecular Psychiatry* to publish articles about vitamin therapy. However, orthomolecular psychiatry never became popular with physicians or authorities on nutrition. There were too many uncertainties and too little research published outside of Hoffer's journal. In 1974 the American Psychiatric Association appointed a Task Force on Vitamin Therapy in Psychiatry. The committee found no scientific basis for orthomolecular psychiatry or megavitamin treatment. They reported that "only acute schizophrenics responded to megavitamin treatment, and their results had been achieved in conjunction with other conventional therapies." (Daniel Raiten, and Thomas Massaro: *Handbook of Autism and Developmental Disorders*, p. 568.)

In *Biology of the Autistic Syndrome*, Dr. Mary Coleman explains why so many people hoped vitamin B_6 or vitamin B_6 with magnesium would help people with autism. She called these supplements "ubiquitous," because they play a role in so many enzymes needed for brain functioning. As the treatment of pellagra showed, the body cannot do without niacin. However, research never proved that people with autism have natural shortages of this nutrient in the brain and body.

Coleman warns us not to expect too much from vitamin treatments because "very few studies have looked for subgroups within the syndrome of biological abnormalities. . . . Since children with many different types of autism were studied as a group, and since the goal was simply to discover some final common pathway or some final mechanism in autism that might explain the symptom complex, these studies are very difficult to interpret." (*Biology of the Autistic Syndrome*, p. 75.)

The leading advocate for megavitamins is neither a medical doctor nor a nutritionist. Bernard Rimland, a psychologist, became an early enthusiast of megavitamin therapy. In 1973 he published a survey of children who received five different mineral or vitamin supplements twice a day. When skeptics questioned Rimland's first report, he undertook another study in 1978.

In the *Handbook of Autism and Developmental Disorders*, Raiten and Massaro write,

> For the study as a whole, there were no consistent differences between Vitamin B6 and placebo phases in

the Rimland et al. (1978) study. The authors did find a difference based on comparisons between the first group, who received the placebo first, and the second group, who received Vitamin B6 first. Four of the six autistic children showed improvements. Although these results, like those of earlier studies, are intriguing, they are equivocal at best and do not furnish the kind of evidence that warrants a mass application of this treatment for all autistic children.

Nearly fifteen years later, people still question the value of megavitamin therapy. Few medical doctors or nutritionists recommend this treatment. However, Dr. Rimland keeps extensive information on this topic and continues to publish positive reports in his newsletter. Parents who want to try this treatment should read his earlier articles or contact him at his office in San Diego (Autism Research Review International).

How does diet affect behavior?

To some extent, diet influences everyone's behavior. We act differently when we're hungry than when we're digesting a large meal. We need protein in our diet, but we digest it slowly. Carbohydrates, on the other hand, give us quick energy. For a really fast start, many people want sugar and caffeine at breakfast.

We develop habits centered around diet and personal beliefs about food. When we associate a food with discomfort we avoid it, whether we have scientific evidence or not. Our choices are personal, psychological, and not necessarily supported by biological research. As adults we have the freedom to make our own food choices, but our children do not. They depend on parents for a healthy, satisfying diet.

Every doctor has advice about children's nutritional needs, but very few think diet affects children with autism differently than others. Research has never proven a connection between nutrition and this disability. However, many parents continue to look for a connection between their child's behavior and certain foods. Some think they have found one.

It's impossible to disprove a family's claim about their child's reaction to a food or drug. They are in the best position to observe that child, around the clock, and in different settings. Almost any response could occur with a single individual. That's why medical researchers insist on reviewing the reactions of many patients before they accept the claims for any drug or diet.

Journals published by nutritionists and medical societies won't publish information on new treatments until their editors and other professional reviewers have examined the evidence. However, commercial publishers tend to print books for their market value, not their medical value. There will always be a market for books that claim diet can make our children smarter, healthier, or better behaved. But few of these books will stand up to their claims.

Some writers recommend eliminating sugar and every type of artificial flavoring, dye, or preservative from food. Some diets even ban foods grown with commercial fertilizers and pesticides. Believers claim that children need organically grown produce to control their behaviors. Skeptics (including most professional nutritionists) say that the body can't recognize the difference between organically grown products and commercial ones.

What about the strange appetites of some people with autism?

Some people with autism have unusual food likes or dislikes. These strange appetites usually don't indicate a nutritional need. A craving for cigarette butts or coffee grounds doesn't mean a child needs nicotine or caffeine in the diet.

More likely, it shows that the person has an unusual response to the taste, maybe even the texture, of foods.

The next chapter will explain that people often crave stimulation in their weakest areas of sense perception. People with low response to pain may pinch or scratch themselves just to awaken the sense of touch. Those who crave the strongest flavors may eat things the rest of us find bitter or repulsive. These unusual eating habits probably indicate a sensory problem, not a nutritional need.

Parents worry about ways to handle problem eating. Some try removing items the child shouldn't eat. They may hide the sugar, quit buying ground coffee, or even avoid sandy beaches. However, avoidance or prohibition might not be the best way to deal with unhealthy habits, for some children simply become more persistent, or even think it's a game to find what's been kept from them.

Try to avoid a power struggle over food. When parents try too hard to control diet, many children rebel, grabbing or sneaking forbidden items. A better approach might be to ration, rather than refuse, certain foods. You could use some foods as part of a reward system. You might also look for healthy substitutes for things your child likes but really shouldn't eat.

When a child wants to eat dangerous or unhealthy items, the parents need to look for substitutes. First, look for a pattern in the person's cravings. Is it taste? Color? Texture? If your youngster's favorite foods share a common feature, offer healthier ones with similar appearance or sensation. Shredded coconut and sunflower seeds have nearly the same texture as ground coffee and they're much more nutritious. Some cheeses have powerful odors. They might repel most children, but appeal to one with an underdeveloped sense of smell. Spices and herbs can strengthen flavors without destroying nutritional value.

Many parents wonder if there is a relationship between their child's food cravings and behavior. Unfortunately, this question hasn't been researched thoroughly. However, in 1983 studies done by Daniel Raiten and Thomas Massaro at Penn State University looked at diet records of forty children with autism and thirty-four typical youngsters. They reported their findings in the *Handbook of Autism and Developmental Disorders:*

> "The autistic group had several different types of eating idiosyncracies, including a higher incidence of food cravings and/or pica [eating of nonfood items such as cigarettes], . . . in 8 out of 21 cases of reported food cravings in the autistic sample, the caregivers reported an association between disturbed behavior and ingestion of the craved food."

Can allergies cause autism?

Vitamin theories blame autism on a lack of nutrients, while allergy theories blame the nutrients themselves. It confuses parents to hear one person say, "Give your child this," and another say, "Take that out of the diet." Which should you believe? Perhaps neither.

Doctors usually don't recommend dietary treatments for autism. Those theories rarely appear in medical publications. When an article does appear in the *Journal of Autism and Developmental Disorders*, the authors usually challenge the diet theory or mention a shortage of scientific evidence. Simply put, the medical profession hasn't found evidence to support dietary treatments for autism. But that hasn't discouraged everyone. People who practice naturopathy believe a natural healing may occur without medicine for every disorder known to man, including autism and cancer.

Naturopathic healers claim they can identify allergenic reactions through a process of fasting, after which foods from different nutritional groups are introduced, one at a time. Naturopaths may have good advice for the average patient, but probably have little information about autism.

After all, even licensed medical doctors consult specialists when diagnosing autism or recommending treatments. People who practice the other healing arts have even less training in developmental disabilities. Most aren't prepared to recognize, evaluate, or treat autism. Chapter 5 has already discussed the difficulty of diagnosing autism.

Many reports of cures hinge on the issue of diagnosis. Saying that diet cured a child is one matter, but proving that he or she actually had autism is another. Mary Callahan faced this challenge. Although trained as a registered nurse, she had very little exposure to autism or other developmental disabilities before the birth of her son, Tony.

When Tony developed learning disabilities and unmanageable behaviors, his doctor diagnosed autism. Callahan accepted the diagnosis, but refused to believe it was incurable. In *Fighting for Tony* (1987) she tells how she searched medical libraries for articles that described behaviors like Tony's. Eventually she read about "cerebral allergies," a theory that claims allergies can disrupt brain functions.

Allergies usually cause mucus accumulation, tissue swelling, and rashes, which often appear as sneezing, asthma, and hives. Allergists can use skin patch tests to diagnose an allergy, or they can eliminate foods from the diet. Callahan tried the second approach and found her son behaved normally when she removed cow's milk and all dairy products from his diet. In 1988, she wrote in the Autism Society of America's *Advocate*:

> "My husband and I didn't know Tony's problem was allergy until we stumbled upon it. We believed he was permanently brain-damaged as the doctors had told us. If I hadn't been a pulmonary nurse working with children with respiratory allergies, I would never have considered removing major allergens from Tony's diet and I never would have seen the eye contact begin, heard the first words spoken or finally had a peaceful night's sleep."

Do Special Diets Help?

Many parents wrote to Callahan after reading her book or seeing her on television. Several believed that allergies had caused their child's autistic symptoms as well. However, single case studies usually aren't accepted as scientific evidence. To reach the skeptics, you need statistics from a documented and controlled study.

The standards of professional research frustrate many parents. Some even accuse doctors and psychologists of hiding information about useful therapies. In 1976, Mary Ackerly, then president of the Autism Society of America, complained that families had to experiment on their own to find useful therapies. She referred to a family's claim that their son's behavior problems were caused by food allergies; ten years before Callahan's book, this family published their story, including details of a five-day fast, in the *Journal of Autism and Childhood Schizophrenia*.

Eric Schopler, editor of the journal, addressed Ackerly's complaint:

> "The President of the Autism Society of America, Mary Ackerly, wrote an enthusiastic introduction to this family's story. Ackerly challenged the professionals, asking why useful therapies were so difficult to 'smoke out.' . . . Judging by the ease with which any intervention claim has access to the popular press, this question should probably be rephrased by asking, 'Why are new therapies difficult to demonstrate as effective?' The main reason for this difficulty is in the highly variable criteria for dissemination."

Simply stated, medical journals don't report on treatments until the editors are satisfied with the scientific evidence, for the simple reason that they don't want parents or doctors to use children as guinea pigs in the mistaken belief that an experimental, untested treatment has the sanction of the wider scientific community. Furthermore, some experiments involve well-documented risks. Making a growing child fast for five days is a dangerous form of child abuse, no matter how well intended the experiment may be.

Why are there so many different opinions on diets?

There are many opinions on this subject because people have different experiences. Unlike medications, which are available only through a physician's prescription, foodstuffs and vitamins are available for anyone to experiment with. Everyone can self-prescribe a diet, for themselves or for their children. The FDA can't regulate home-based experiments, and parents usually don't keep the records needed to publish in a medical journal.

Dr. Morris Lipton, the director of biological research at the University of North Carolina, explains why professionals have doubts about individual's claims of the success of diet therapies:

Large numbers of people are on special diets designed to improve longevity, treat skin conditions, prevent receding hair, or improve their love lives. If these treatments satisfy the consumer and do no harm, they are solely a matter of personal concern. But if they are advocated nationally for medical use, then they must be carefully scrutinized by the medical scientific community.

Mental illness and behavioral disorders of children constitute a special illustration of this problem. . . . The treatments available thus far leave much to be desired. Therefore, new treatments are constantly advocated. One such treatment, which has been offered for more than twenty years, is that of megavitamins. These are reported to help about 50% of the children with childhood schizophrenia, autism, or hyperkinesis. But there is no substantial evidence to support either the theory or the practice.

Lipton suggests that families document their success with unusual therapies by going to NIH (National Institutes of Health) for evaluation. However, he's never convinced a family to take this suggestion because, "They are satisfied with the results of the treatment, do not wish to make a guinea pig out of their child, and do not wish to jeopardize the progress which has been made."

The issue of numbers separates people into two different camps; those who believe a single family's success story, and those who demand a statistical evaluation of several research subjects.

Reliability comes into question when parents report treating a child without professional evaluation and observation. Professionals don't doubt the honesty of those families, merely the objectivity. Do the parents see benefits because they *want* to see them, or because they exist? Was the initial diagnosis even correct?

We all have barriers to total objectivity. Our personal experiences impress us more than those of others. If we see our child improve with a new treatment, it's hard to separate the psychological from the biological effects. The very nature of the relationship between parent and child makes objective observation difficult, because, naturally, the parent wants to see the child improve. Often, the child wants to please the parent. Their interactions may make a bigger difference than the treatment itself.

When a mother serves juice with a pill, her child gets the message, "This is important. Here's something Mom cares enough about to deliver with a bribe." The clue doesn't have to be juice. Other bribes work too. Praise or snuggling on Mom's lap may make a child cooperate with treatment. In scientific language, any of these little extras—changes in routine—are "contaminating variables." They contaminate, or complicate, the experiment because they introduce factors we're not able to measure. A true scientist records every detail in an experiment, behaviors of the therapist as well as those of the child.

When you see improvements during a trial treatment, you

should ask, "What's really causing the changes? Is it the pill, or the procedure?" Professionals routinely ask this question. That's why they give some subjects a powerless pill, called a placebo. *Placebo* comes from Latin and means "I will please." Although useless as a medicine, the placebo has a research value. It shows investigators if the patient's response is biological or psychological. In researcher's language, the placebo guards against the "halo effect," the very human tendency to see what we want to see, believe what we want to believe.

Are there any risks in experimenting with diets?

Chances are, if you consult naturopaths or other health food advocates, they'll suggest changes in your child's diet. Any supplements they recommend are probably harmless, possibly even helpful. However, you shouldn't make a child fast as part of a dietary experiment. It's always dangerous to remove basic nutrients from the diet, especially for growing children. Your child needs a balanced diet, including proteins, carbohydrates, and modest amounts of fat. A nutritionist can tell you if the child is getting enough of the essential vitamins and minerals.

Foodstuffs and diet supplements have fewer side effects than man-made drugs. Most vitamins can't harm a person, even when taken in enormous quantities. Water-soluble vitamins, like niacin and vitamin B, don't build up to toxic levels in the body. They're quickly processed and pass through the system in a few days. On the other hand, a few fat-soluble vitamins, such as vitamin A, are stored in vital organs and can prove harmful if they become too concentrated in the body.

Parents should consider the psychological, behavioral, and social consequences of a diet. Everyone who lives with the child may be affected by the change in diet. When you decide to eliminate items from the diet, will you make everyone in the family give up the sugar or the food additives? Or will you let other family members consume what they want in front of the child with autism? Will meals become a time of jealousy, or a time when everyone resents the loss of favorite foods?

Changes in diet can start a power struggle between parent and child. Children may rebel, have tantrums, or search out forbidden treats. The conflict between a demanding child and a controlling parent can become a losing situation for both parties. It helps to offer new treats in place of the ones removed from the diet. Some diets let you limit, rather than eliminate, favorite foods.

Behaviorists know that food choices can be powerful motivators. Parents might ask, "Is it worth it to experiment with diets that might make my child rebel? Or is it better to negotiate, using those foods as part of a reward system?" The family has to decide if a diet offers enough benefits to justify frustrating the youngster with autism. Unless you have sound evidence that a food actually causes a negative physical reaction, it's probably not worth your trouble to ration it or eliminate it.

Finally, parents should consider the social consequences of an unusual diet. Children miss social and recreational opportunities when they can't eat foods served at school, at camp, or at McDonald's. Ask, "What evidence exists to support the claims for this diet?" Then weigh those odds against the family's inconvenience and the child's stress.

REVIEW

The neurological system, not the digestive system, causes autism. Scientific studies have never proven a link between autism and diet. However, in the 1960s, a few individuals proposed treating mental illness and developmental disabilities with vitamins. This theory, called orthomolecular psychiatry, was never endorsed by nutritionists.

A number of parents still try megavitamin treatments for a child with autism. Some are satisfied with these treatments, but their success stories are hard to evaluate. Expectations vary from family to family, and the children have different symptoms and behaviors. It's therefore hard to know what individuals mean when they call a treatment successful. Medical scientists expect more specific evidence and evaluation than families generally provide.

Some diet books blame hyperactivity on sugar or food additives. However, these claims aren't accepted by most doctors and nutritionists. No evidence exists to show that people with autism react to nutrients differently than the rest of us.

Many people with autism crave unusual foods, or even eat nonfood items such as cigarette butts or sand. These habits probably have nothing to do with nutritional differences but indicate sensory differences. A person with an unusual response to taste, aroma, or texture may seek sensations the rest of us find unappetizing or repulsive.

For many years people have discussed the theory that food allergies cause autism. A few families claim they've found foods that triggered the symptoms of autism. None of these claims have been supported by scientific review. For example, author Mary Callahan (*Fighting for Tony*) admits that she didn't "cure" her son of autism. He had been misdiagnosed. Allergy treatments just eliminated behaviors formerly mistaken for symptoms of autism.

People will always debate diet treatments because there will always be children with new diagnoses and parents who try every treatment they hear about. A few children will improve during one experiment, and others will seem to benefit from another.

Parents are usually right when they say their child has made progress. But scientists are bound to ask the awkward questions: What made the child improve: diet, changes in mealtime routine, or some other factor? Did the new diet have any effect, or was the child ready to move forward according to his own developmental calendar?

It's probably safe to experiment with alternative foods and vitamin supplements. However, it's dangerous to withhold basic nutrients or make a young child fast. Get the opinion of a trusted doctor or professional nutritionist before fasts or allergy treatments. If someone suggests a diet for your child, ask him or her to explain the theory. Then, check it out with a nutritionist or your doctor. Many of the unproven diet theories assume that a lot of a good thing is better than a little. Nutritional researchers don't support this belief. They tell us the body can't use the excess amounts of these nutrients. Surplus water-soluble vitamins just pass through the urine, and extra protein is converted to fat by the body.

What else should I read?

Callahan, Mary. *Fighting for Tony*. New York: Simon & Schuster, 1987.

Coleman, Mary, M.D., and Gillberg, Christopher. *Biology of the Autistic Syndrome*. New York: Praeger, 1985.

Cohen, Donald, M.D., and Donnellan, Anne. *Handbook of Autism and Developmental Disorders*. New York: Wiley, 1987.

Rimland, Bernard. *Autism Research Review International*. Autism Research Institute, 4182 Adams Avenue, San Diego, CA 92116.

9

Do Exercise and Physical Therapies Help?

Occupational therapy and exercise make tremendous contributions to the individualized education plan. These therapies shouldn't take the student's time and energy away from other educational goals, but instead become a part of them. The right program uses sensory integration to make the rest of the school day more productive.

Absolutely! Exercise is as important to human health as nutrition. In fact, physical therapies and exercise may offer people with autism more help than any dietary or medical treatment. However, like nutrients and medication, exercise works best when used in moderation.

Some children with autism need more physical stimulation than the average child. Others can't tolerate certain sensations. Occupational therapists can help parents understand their child's physical needs and choose appropriate exercises and forms of play. A well-chosen physical program may improve the child's behavior, self-control, and learning.

We don't know exactly how physical therapies affect individuals with autism. Neurological development, sense of balance, and coordination vary from person to person. Everyone gets some benefits from exercise: better metabolism, cardiovascular efficiency, more regular bowel movements—in other words, "general good health." But, exercise affects people with neurological disorders more than the typical person. It's well documented that regular exercise reduces stress and lowers blood pressure. Some physicians believe there's a relationship between the stress reduction and the endorphins the body produces during an activity such as jogging. Perhaps we'll discover other benefits in the future.

Exercise and physical treatments have a long and varied history. Many cultures developed practices such as cold baths, saunas, even marathons. Some customs, like rocking a baby to sleep or wrapping infants in swaddling clothes to quiet them, are so old their origins are lost to us, and we merely do them because they seem to work. These traditions seem to be based on primitive human needs that modern neurologists and occupational therapists are just beginning to research.

The ancient Greeks didn't have biological research, but they believed in a connection between physical and mental development. From kindergarten on, physical education classes continue this tradition. Yet, one of the most interesting uses of physical education comes not from our Western heritage, but from Japan.

What is Daily Life Therapy?

This term is translated from the Japanese word, *higashi*. Dr. Kiyo Kitahara, chose this name to describe the educational program she developed for children with autism. By the early eighties, Kitahara's first school had earned an international reputation (see Chapter 13, "What's the Best Approach to Education?").

Eventually, parents in the United States persuaded Kitahara to start a school in this country, and in 1987, she opened the Boston Higashi School. Finally, Western-trained teachers had a chance to observe this Japanese program.

The Americans found many different practices, but none impressed them more than Kitahara's emphasis on exercise.

In 1989, the *Journal of Autism and Developmental Disorders* published Dr. Kathleen Quill's review of the Boston Higashi School. Quill considered exercise the most practical contribution of the Kitahara program. More time spent in organized exercise, she pointed out, meant less time for pointless self-stimulatory activity. At the Higashi School, students never have the time or privacy for repetitious, autistic behaviors.

Quill suggested that exercise might have other benefits explained by medical research. She mentioned the work of Dr. Paul Hardy, a Boston physician who had earned a reputation for research in neurology and autism.

Dr. Hardy agreed to serve as medical consultant to the Boston Higashi School. Hardy and others hoped to compare their view of autism with Kitahara's. On a theoretical level, they had little in common. Kitahara's beliefs were firmly rooted in Japanese tradition. Group activity and conformity were stressed throughout the school day, with students wearing uniforms and attending classes six days a week. However, the exercise program seemed adaptable to American education models. Quill offered this description:

Daily Life Therapy incorporates the use of vigorous physical exercise as a central feature of the curriculum. The program of intense physical exercise, dominated by running, appears to function as a means to decrease the children's undesirable behaviors by the natural release of beta-endorphins, and therefore, facilitates the child's ability to attend and learn. During the first months in the program, children ran outside for twenty minutes, 2–3 times a day. Children who are resistant to running are physically guided through the running course by an adult. An additional daily gym period includes gymnastics, aerobic exercises, and martial arts. The children engage in outside play for another hour, which involves soccer, basketball, biking, and climbing on play equipment. For the preschool children, the rigor of the exercise program is modified. Long walks are substituted for running and regular playground equipment is used for outside play. Their gym activities include roller skating, biking, and sprinting, along with movement games requiring motor imitation.

Today a number of teachers follow part of Kitahara's exercise program. No one copies her gymnastic routines, but many believe that running for twenty to thirty minutes helps their students. Teachers often report that children pay more attention to schoolwork after their exercise period.

What is holding therapy?

Chapter 3 explains that modern knowledge about autism has discredited many earlier beliefs about it, along with most early forms of therapy. However, one technique seems to have value, though not for the reasons originally claimed.

In the 1960s and early 1970s some professionals practiced a technique called holding therapy, based on the belief that autism occurred because the child failed to bond with the mother during infancy. Therapists believed that an intense physical contact between parent and child would overcome the autism and let the child begin a more normal life.

Dr. Martha Welch and others who practiced holding therapy claimed they could cure autism. However, they never produced evidence, so the treatment remained controversial. The neurological discoveries of the 1980s made holding therapy seem as obsolete as belief in a flat earth. However, there were still unsolved questions, still pieces missing in the puzzle of autism.

Occupational therapists understand that infants and some other people crave stimulation of the proprioceptive system. Proprioception is the sense that tells us the position and location of our body parts, sort of a sensory map of our body that aids in awareness of self and well-being. This sense helps us, literally, to know where we are in this physical world and to move through it with more ease and confidence.

Proprioceptive stimulation includes binding, swaddling, and other forms of deep pressure. One way to apply deep pressure is to hug or squeeze a person. When mothers embrace their children, they're giving proprioceptive stimulation as well as affection. Gentle pressure from the mother's arms delivers a physical message. The child senses, "I am here, she is around me. Her touch lets me feel that I have a back, a front, and arms on each side."

While the "holding therapists" didn't base their treatment on the principle of proprioceptive stimulation, their techniques calmed some of their subjects. In other words, they may have done the right thing for the wrong reason!

Some children with autism seem to crave deep-pressure stimulation. Temple Grandin recalls one of her childhood activities: "I used to get under the sofa cushions and have my sister sit on them. Pressure had a very calming and relaxing effect."

She also liked crawling into snug, nestlike places. At one time, a Freudian analyst might have called this a yearning for the womb. But we describe these behaviors in biological terms today.

What's a "hug machine?"

Beginning in childhood, Grandin realized that certain activities could calm her and help her concentrate. As she grew older, she recognized a pattern and sought out new experiences to soothe her. Eventually, she found one in an unlikely place!

During a visit to an aunt's ranch, Grandin watched the cattle's reaction to a squeeze chute. The device was designed to hold animals firmly, but gently, during veterinary procedures. Temple was fascinated. She noticed a side effect of the cattle chute; the animals seemed to relax during the process. She wondered how the cattle chute would feel to her, so she crawled in.

Grandin remembers, "After a horrible bout of the nerves, I got in the squeeze chute. For about 45 minutes I was much calmer. I then built a squeeze-chute-like device, which I could use to apply any pressure (which I controlled). When I first used the machine I had a tendency to pull away from the pressure because the stimulation was overwhelming. Gradually, my overly-sensitive nervous system became habilitated and I could relax and enjoy the soothing pressure." Eventually Grandin realized that people besides herself might find relief from a hug machine. She has produced more of these machines and offers these guidelines for their use:

A) Let the individual control the amount of pressure and the length of time in the chute.
B) Don't force an individual into this device. However, some individuals will need a lot of gentle encouragement to get them to start using the machine.
C) Let the individual use the machine as desired, any time, as much or as little as desired.

Researchers at the Michael Reese Hospital and Medical Center in Chicago have studied children's use of the hug machine since 1986. Margaret Creedon, Ph.D., and Grace Baraek have begun research on ways the hug machine may be used in a classroom. They have already observed how often children initiated its use, the length of time spent in the machine, and the amount of pressure each child chose to receive. This research should eventually help us understand which types of students crave this stimulation and the type of improvements we should look for.

What's the difference between occupational therapy and physical therapy?

These terms confuse many parents, especially when they meet both a PT and an OT when they attend the annual Individual Education Plan (IEP) meeting at their child's school. The law requires that every professional involved with the IEP be available for the parents to ask questions. Be sure to ask!

The roles of physical therapy and occupational therapy seem so similar that they can confuse many families. Physical therapists use massage, exercise, and other physical remedies to help students develop strength and coordination. Many of the physical therapist's suggestions relate to the playground or use of exercise equipment. The term *occupational therapy* is misleading, because people generally associate *occupation* with work or employment. In the field of therapy, however, the term covers a wide variety of activities, things that "occupy" people. When an OT attends a five-year-old's IEP meeting, it's not to plan the youngster's career, but rather to evaluate the child's progress in neuromotor and physical functions.

Occupational therapists know that unusual childhood behaviors often indicate a delay in neurological development. They look at sensory and physical responses as signs of developmental progress. When an infantile behavior lasts too long, an OT knows it may signal a neurological problem.

Our neurological system lets us cope with a multisensory environment by selectively turning our attention to just a few signals from the baffling array of sights, sounds, and sensations in our environment. Meanwhile, the brain must screen out a huge number of distracting sensations so that we may concentrate on those that concern us. We're not born with that ability, however.

Newborns aren't fully comfortable in a world of light, sound, and thermal change. It takes a while to adjust after nine months in a closed, confined space. That first environment—the womb—wasn't stable either; it shifted this way and that every time the mother moved. The unborn child had no control of motion or balance and no sense of those either, for a very good reason. If the fetus had a sense of balance, it would grow dizzy to the point of nausea. However, nature protects the unborn by delaying key neurological developments. The sense of balance, for example, doesn't develop until well after birth.

During infancy, children develop in ways we can't easily observe, gaining a sense of balance, of space, and of self, for example. Neurological problems, such as autism, often interfere with this development. This may not be noticeable to others, however, until the child shows delay in more obvious skills, such as talking or hand-eye coordination.

What can these therapies do?

Occupational therapists study the physical systems used in different activities or "occupations." Even simple behaviors require more than muscular development: an individual has to coordinate skeletal-muscular movement with sensory signals, such as sight and sound. The therapist may say, "Clap your hands," setting off a series of responses for the child: hear the command, interpret its meaning, send the command on to the neurons that control the motor actions of the body.

The quality of sensory input will shape an individual's performance in various activities. If sensory information isn't processed, a person may not respond to stimuli at all. Milder sensory disturbances can cause clumsiness, confusion, and general developmental delay.

Sensory information depends on more than the five senses. The eyes may see, the ears may hear, but their messages have to pass through neurological circuits that interpret them to become meaningful to a person. When problems occur along the neurological pathways, even the most important information from the organs may become useless or distracting to the individual. This is considered a problem of sensory integration, because signals from the different senses don't produce a coordinated or synthesized message in the brain. It may seem like the person is viewing one television channel, while hearing a different one. Confusing or unrecognized signals from the senses simply won't relay valid information on to the other parts of the mind responsible for judgment, decision, and action.

Occupational therapists play a key role in diagnosis and assessment of neurological disabilities. They examine an individual's skills in terms of the underlying sensory and physical development. A child's reaction to spinning, bouncing, or balancing lets an OT evaluate his neurological development. Then, the therapist will target areas of delay for appropriate exercise and therapy.

Parents often record their child's development through photos and a "Baby's Book." These family documents can be very helpful when professionals ask at what age a child first showed a behavior and at what point he or she outgrew it. The toddler's response to light, sound, and motion, often captured on camera, marks developmental milestones, visible evidence that sensory information is being analyzed and then used to emerge as a new behavior like sitting up or walking.

Can we treat sensory problems?

Occupational therapists call people who overreact to common sensations sensory defensive. It's appropriate to feel pain in response to strong stimuli; that's part of our human survival system. Children learn to avoid fire and other dangers because their senses warn them through pain. However, neurological problems can make harmless sensations disturbing or frightening. A few children find clothing uncomfortable, conversation distracting, and the smell of some foods repulsive. Temple Grandin found some clothing unbearable, "Scratchy petticoats were like sandpaper rubbing on raw nerve endings."

When simple everyday events upset or frighten a child, it can trigger many of the symptoms of autism, including screaming at certain sounds, irrational fears, even withdrawal from other people. Instead of forcing the child to "behave" or "act normal," we should investigate the reasons behind the child's behavior. Does this youngster find common sensations disturbing?

Patricia and Julia Wilbarger, registered occupational therapists (OTRs) have coauthored a pamphlet, "Sensory Defensiveness in Children Aged 2–12." They explain that sensory defensiveness may appear in mild, moderate, or severe degrees. The severity of the problem will determine many of a child's behaviors:

Children with mild defensiveness often appear "picky." They may fuss about food or clothes and get easily irritated. Some, like Temple Grandin, do well in school. But, as the Wilbargers note, it may take "enormous control and effort to succeed in these areas." If they can't maintain the necessary level of control, they risk emotional crisis.

Children with moderate sensory defensiveness are usually affected in two or more basic life areas. They are socially affected, often choosing isolation or showing forms of aggression. They may also have delayed self-care skills, including toilet training, in addition to attention problems at school.

The Wilbargers' description of severe sensory defensiveness will strike a familiar note for many readers: "These children usually have other diagnostic labels for various areas of dysfunction (i.e., severe developmental delay, autism, autistic-like behavior or emotionally disturbed). Strong avoidance of some kinds of sensations or the reverse, intense sensory seeking are common."

Children with severe sensory defensiveness appear the hardest to teach, even untrainable. Some will put gravel, or even broken glass, into their mouths. One might attempt to smell other people's body odors, or play with her own feces. The possibilities are almost endless. These sensory problems can make a child crave the strongest forms of stimulation, or flee from the mildest.

An occupational therapist can help the parents and teachers set priorities for an individual child. First, the therapist will do an assessment of the child's sensory responses, then choose appropriate therapeutic activities. Treating the sensory defensiveness first makes the other forms of intervention more effective.

What is Sensory Integration Therapy?

Sensory integration therapy uses physical activities to help people regulate their response to different sensory systems. First, the therapists look at observable behaviors, such as posture, movement, or response to touch. Does the child alternate from left to right foot while climbing stairs, or does he always advance with the same foot and draw the other one behind? How old was the little girl when she began showing a preference for left hand or right hand? Will the youngster sit upright during a class activity, or slowly tilt to the side?

Registered occupational therapists are trained to recognize those childrens' behaviors that indicate that a sensory or motor system needs attention. Their training prepares them to recognize problems that include balance (vestibular system), awareness of body position (proprioceptive system), and touch (tactile system).

After identifying the specific problems, the therapist chooses activities that will help the individual "integrate" information from the senses with particular body experiences. Examples may include massage, firm touch, or spinning, rocking, and bouncing. Fortunately, this therapy can take the form of play, so a child can have sensory integration therapy while enjoying a recreational or social activity.

Lorna Jean King explained the goals of sensory integration in a guest editorial for *Autism Research Review International*:

> First, therapists look for activities that will make the student calm and alert. Once the child feels comfortable, he or she can pay better attention to the learning activities that follow.
>
> Next, the therapist helps the child associate sensation with information. Playful activities can make children more aware of their bodies, movement, and space. Those physical experiences give learners sensory feedback and become an important source of information.
>
> Finally, sensory integration teaches concepts such as *over*, under, *fast*, and *slow*. Students need to understand these terms before they can grasp other concepts, such as space, speed, and pressure. This information prepares learners for later lessons that teach functional skills at school, play, or work; hence the term *occupational therapy*.

How much is enough?

Amateurs and unqualified therapists sometimes make the mistake of thinking that if a little is good, a lot will be better. This simply isn't true when it comes to occupational or physical therapies. Lorna Jean King recommends a "diet of needed sensory motor experiences." She means that, like a nutritional diet, these activities should occur in small, regular doses. Used properly, sensory integration makes the rest of the school day more productive.

Sensory integration therapy may take only a few minutes of time per activity. Temple Grandin believes in letting individuals choose how long and how often they will participate in a particular activity, but some direction from the therapist is required with children who have avoidance reactions to touching.

The therapist must be gently insistent and encourage touching. Deep pressure should be used because it calms the nervous system. Light touch tends to excite the nervous system. It's extremely important that the child's therapy be planned by a registered occupational therapist. A certified therapist, teacher, aide, or parent may be able to carry out the daily therapy, once designed, but they shouldn't try to design the basic routine. Poorly chosen therapies can backfire, arousing a youngster you want to calm, or sedating one you'd rather stimulate. These activities are supposed to fine tune a neurological system that's out of focus. A random manipulation of the system won't help the student or the teacher.

Dr. Creedon's studies of Grandin's hug machine show that children varied in their use of it and other proprioceptive therapies. However, none chose to use the machine longer than two and a half minutes, or more than a few times a day. Temple Grandin, recalling her own experiences as a child with autism, warns us, "All therapeutic activities should be done as fun games." Avoid "too much of a good thing" with exercise and physical therapies for a growing child.

Are any physical therapies harmful?

Registered professionals in the fields of occupational therapy and physical therapy have high standards for training and licensing personnel. As in the field of nutrition, students have to complete a series of complicated courses and pass examinations before they're licensed to practice. Their work may look simple—playing with children, scheduling exercises, or recommending diets—but years of scientific research went into that professional's training.

Perhaps a therapist is so skillful that her work looks easy; maybe you wouldn't know she had years of training unless you saw it on paper. It's hard for most of us to appreciate the complicated scientific principles behind some therapies. Unfortunately, it's also hard for us to tell when a theory lacks scientific evidence—or is simply fraudulent.

Some treatments sound scientific in their ads and promotional literature, but actually misrepresent medical research. Such therapies may harm more than they help. For over a decade responsible organizations such as the American Academy of Pediatrics have tried to warn parents about the Doman-Delacato Patterning Technique promoted through the Institutes for the Achievement of Human Potential in Philadelphia.

Glenn Doman claims his program can reduce, even cure, neurological problems in children. His treatment includes a radical and unorthodox diet plus a demanding program of exercise and physical therapy called patterning. Parents and volunteers try to "pattern" the child's neuromotor pathways by moving the youngster's limbs through a series of exercises.

In 1981, Dr. Edward Zigler, professor of psychology at Yale, complained that Doman had raised unrealistic hopes in many parents, but added, "I know of no accounts relating the experiences of families some time after they have assayed or completed the treatment."

Eight years later, Zigler had his chance. Berneen Bratt invited him to write the introduction to her book, *No Time for Jello*, in which she describes years of stress and fatigue, following the program she thought would help a son with cerebral palsy. Her experience resembles that of other parents, including many who have a child with autism. None of these families can claim a cure, in spite of incredible effort, commitment, and inconvenience.

"This is a cautionary tale showing how and why a middle-class educated family could fall victim to a therapy that doesn't work," Zigler writes in the introduction. "The book powerfully evokes the emotional ups and downs associated with any therapy."

In *Mixed Blessings*, Barbara and William Christopher share their experience with the Doman program. They explain that the staff told them their seven-year-old son should be allowed to walk only one hour a day. The rest of the time he had to crawl and follow an exhausting schedule that included breathing exercises, patterning, and studying flash cards prepared by his mother.

The Christophers invested tremendous amounts of time, energy, and money in this program, but after three years, they lost hope and began looking for a residential program for their son. The parents finally burned out, and their son's behavior indicates he may have felt that way too.

In 1982 the American Academy of Pediatrics's policy statement on the Doman-Delacato Program recommended: "Physicians and therapists should acquaint themselves with the issues in the controversy and the available evidence. Based on past and current analysis, studies, and reports, we must conclude that patterning treatment offers no special merit, that the claims of its advocates are unproven, and that the demands on families are so great that in some cases there may be harm in its use."

REVIEW

The neurological problems behind autism can affect a person's response to physical sensations in ways we may not fully understand. Over the years, a number of approaches have been tried, and theories have ranged from Freudian views of infantile regression to sensory damage.

Daily Life Therapy, developed by Dr. Kiyo Kitahara of Tokyo, introduced strenuous exercise into the school curriculum as a way of increasing students' attention to academic tasks. Western researchers assume that the body's endorphins, released during exercise, explain some of these benefits.

Temple Grandin taught us the calming effects of deep-pressure stimulation, first through her autobiography, and then by inventing the hug machine, which lets children control their own proprioceptive therapy.

Researchers have long known that people with autism

have unusual reactions to different sensory experiences. Occupational therapists have turned this knowledge to practical use. They can tell a lot about children's neurological development by watching them during activities that involve stimulation of the vestibular, proprioceptive, or tactile senses. Therapists then plan sensory integration activities to help youngsters cope with some of their neurological problems.

Occupational therapists recommend activities that take only a few minutes a day and can be worked into other social or recreational experiences. They believe a little physical therapy may be more effective than too much.

Parents must guard against therapies that sound promising but do not have legitimate scientific evidence to support their claims. The Doman-Delacato Patterning program, promoted through the Institutes for the Achievement of Human Potential, has been condemned by physicians and registered therapists for years, but some families can't resist trying a program that promises a cure, no matter how many professionals tell them that promise is false.

What else should I read?

American Academy of Pediatrics. "Policy Statement: The Doman-Delacato Treatment of Neurologically Handicapped Children." *Pediatrics*, Vol. 70, No. 5 (Nov. 1982).

Bratt, Berneen. *No Time for Jello*. Cambridge, Mass.: Brookline Books, 1989.

Christopher, Barbara and William. *Mixed Blessings*. Nashville: Abingdon Press, 1989.

Creedon, Margaret and Baraek, Grace. "Developmentally Disabled Children's Use of Lateral Pressure Equipment: Day

School Report." (1990) Developmental Institute, Michael Reese Hospital and Medical Center, Chicago.

Grandin, Temple, with Scariano, M.: *Emergence: Labeled Autistic*. Novato, CA: Arena Press, 1986.

Sensory Integration Quarterly. Sensory Integration International, 1402 Cravens Avenue, Torrance, CA 90501-2701.

10

Are There Any Therapies for Sensory Disorders?

Medical science has taken different directions in the diagnosis and treatment of disorders of the five sensory systems. The technological approaches are as different as the senses themselves. However, there's a common principle behind the treatment of any of these sensory disorders: identify the sensory problem and try to adjust that system so that the individual has a better chance to perceive his or her world as we perceive ours.

Since Leo Kanner made his first checklist of symptoms associated with autism, we have known to look for unusual responses to sound. Testing for hearing loss is still one of the first steps in diagnosis. Fifty years into our research of autism, we are finding more and more evidence that senses other than hearing are also involved.

The clinical results of sensory integration therapy suggest that sensory abnormalities may be too important to merely list among other symptoms, such as learning disabilities and behavior problems; sensory difficulties may actually cause the other symptoms! In other words, the irrational fears, the indifference to environmental danger, the difficulties with communication—all key symptoms in the detection of autism—might simply indicate that the child has a disorder that distorts his or her perception of sight, sound, or touch.

Occupational therapists, as mentioned in the last chapter, claim no miraculous cures, but they follow tested principles of sensory therapy: either to desensitize an overactive response or to increase sensitivity in an underactive area.

When therapists accurately identify an overactive sense, the process of treatment is fairly clear: gradually introduce stimulation, through playful activity, until the child shows tolerance or acceptance of the mildest form of that sensation. A child who screams at the touch of carpets or upholstery might agree to play with a ball, even accepting a rough-textured tennis ball. If the therapy proceeds at the child's pace, without forcing him to encounter the things he tries to avoid, the youngster may eventually graduate to an acceptance of more textured materials. A healing hasn't necessarily occurred. The child may still have stronger-than-average responses to the sensation, but he's learned enough tolerance of the stimulant to let his family carpet the home and use fabric upholstery instead of smooth plastic.

The opposite of desensitization, of course, is sensitization. Children who ignore or overlook some types of stimulation may sometimes be trained to pay attention. The game strategy, as Temple Grandin recalls from her own childhood, works best. If the child discovers a fun reward or reinforcement through the senses, he or she will pay more attention the next time the stimulant appears. The ears perk up when the listener knows a bell will signal time for dessert!

We sensitize ourselves when we become connoisseurs of the things we like. Wine tasters, cooks, hobbyists of every type, hone their tastes through exposure to their interests. Most people can increase their sensitivity through recreation, but people with autism cannot control their own sensitization or desensitization. They need our help.

What is auditory training?

Sound of a Miracle, published in 1991, is probably the most remarkable account of sensory therapy ever told. In her book, Annabel Stehli tells a story that begins with a quest familiar to many families of children disabled by autism. She tells of years spent following every lead, looking for a treatment for her daughter Georgiana.

Mrs. Stehli tried everything—even religions that promised miraculous intervention—to help Georgiana. Eventually, the mother became resigned, assuming that her daughter would never overcome her learning disabilities and antisocial behaviors. However, the family moved to Europe in 1976, and an unexpected opportunity appeared. Stehli heard about a therapy for hearing disorders. This treatment, called auditory training, was unknown to parents in the United States and might remain unknown today if it weren't for the attention brought by Stehli's book.

Stehli made an appointment with a doctor in Geneva who was known to treat people with disorders related to hearing. She discussed Georgiana's developmental history and her reactions to certain sounds with the doctor. She explained his response: "He would do a detailed audiogram, which would reveal the exact frequencies where her distortions occurred. He said he would then retrain her hearing at these points. The treatment would take only half an hour, twice a day, for ten days."

According to Stehli, her daughter began showing dramatic progress within five days after starting auditory training. She learned to tolerate sounds such as rainfall, surf, and wind, that had formerly frightened her.

Within a short amount of time, the mother realized her daughter's conversation had improved, because she was finally paying attention to dialog. Eventually, she asked her mother, "Can you teach me how to act normal?" An ecstatic Stehli ends the book with a series of boasts: her daughter enrolled in regular schools, graduated, won honors in college, and married.

This story appealed to everyone who had pursued treatment for a "hopeless" disorder, making *Sound of a Miracle* the best selling book about autism since Barry Kaufman's *Son-Rise* and *A Miracle to Believe In. Reader's Digest* printed excerpts before the book arrived in stores and talk shows all over the country tried to schedule the mother and daughter for appearances.

Leading authorities on autism became interested in the Stehli's experience. Temple Grandin met Georgiana and asked her exactly what benefits she thought she'd received from auditory training. "It fixed my ears," she replied. Many professionals admitted knowing that hearing disorders frequently affected people with autism, but they had never expected to see such dramatic benefits from desensitization therapy.

Predictably, thousands of parents rushed to make appointments for their children to be seen by auditory trainers. Overnight, a new industry was born. Stehli founded the Georgiana Foundation to provide information about the therapy and to schedule training seminars. Entrepreneurs purchased equipment, took training, and began marketing their services.

How does it work?

Dr. Bernard Rimland, publisher of *Autism Research Review International*, has always encouraged parents to try anything that might help a child with autism. Discovering that there was virtually no published research on auditory training, Rimland offered to design the world's first research project on the subject.

The Center for the Study of Autism in Oregon is the site of Rimland's research on auditory training. Dr. Stephen Edelson, director of the center, offers this description of the theory behind auditory training:

In general, we know that many people with autism have auditory processing problems. Researchers around the world have examined brain waves in people with autism and have found that these individuals do not seem to process auditory information normally. In addition, many people with autism exhibit a negative reaction to some sounds in their environment.

At this time, we do not know why people may benefit from auditory training. Dr. [Guy] Berard states that some people with auditory processing problems hear some frequencies much better than other frequencies. When people have auditory peaks, they hear in a distorted manner and may find it difficult to make sense out of their auditory world. Dr. Berard feels that auditory training normalizes a person's hearing so the person hears all frequencies equally well. This is accomplished by placing filters on those frequencies in which the person hears exceptionally well. The filters block out those specific frequencies, and the person does not hear these sounds during auditory training sessions.

This is only a theory. One of my theories is based on Dr. Eric Courchesne's research, showing that people with autism have difficulty shifting their attention from one stimulus to another stimulus. Since auditory training involves presenting low and high frequency sounds at random, the trainee is constantly shifting his or her attention back and forth. Thus, auditory training might be training the trainee to shift attention. This may explain why many parents report an increase in both listening and attention in their children. And when people attend, they learn.

Another theory of auditory training is that since low and high frequency sounds are sent at random, the trainee cannot anticipate them; and as a result, the trainee cannot "tune-out" the sounds; thus, the person is being taught to "tune-in" to his or her environment.

Edelson concludes: "These are just a few theories that make sense, and there are several more out there." Among the theories he doesn't mention is that of Dr. Alfred Tomatis, who developed a similar technique forty years ago, proposing to re-bond the child with the mother, believing the child may have been unwanted and, thus, deprived of a sonic link with the mother during pregnancy."

You won't find a clearer explanation of auditory training until the Center for the Study of Autism is ready to issue its first reports. There simply is no evidence to support any of these theories at this time. We could say that auditory training is a treatment in search of a theory, but most parents don't really care. Few care *how* it works, they just want to see *if* it works!

Who can benefit from auditory training?

Annabel Stehli has said she believed the training would work best with individuals similar to her daughter, people she would call high-functioning who also have sensory input disorders. However, Dr. Edelson has seen people he considered low-functioning respond to the therapy. Temple Grandin holds yet another view, suggesting that auditory training benefits people who have language in early childhood, but later regress. "At this point," Edelson admits, "we can't predict who will benefit from auditory training."

The problem of predicting *who* will benefit can't really be solved until we define *what* benefits to expect. This will be hard to answer until the auditory trainers agree on a theory to explain what the treatment actually does for an individual. If it merely desensitizes a person's hearing, in which case we would expect individuals to appear calmer and more controlled while exposed to sounds that formerly bothered them, that's enough to make the therapy worthwhile. If it trains people to pay better attention and show a greater ability to focus on environmental stimuli, we should see more people make leaps in communication, like Georgiana reportedly made.

Thousands of people have already had this treatment, yet no one has published a survey of results. Virtually all of the information to date is anecdotal, but it appears that most parents have been enthusiastic. For example, one mother mentioned that after her daughter had auditory training, the family could use household appliances again. The girl no longer shrieked at the sound of the blender, the vacuum, or the VCR while it rewound. That's certainly a benefit to the family, if not to the child as well.

The concept behind auditory training makes sense, even if we don't understand how it works. As mentioned before, abnormal response to sound is one of the most common, as well as the earliest, symptoms of autism. Anything that desensitizes the child to painful or distracting sounds would make life more pleasant for the youngster and the people she lives with.

Dr. Edelson has said, "I don't want people to get the impression that we are promoting auditory training. If, in our second study, we find that auditory training is not effective, I will not hesitate sharing these results. Some people have told me that we are wasting our time conducting research, and everyone should just try auditory training. If it works, great!!; and if it doesn't work, then not much is lost. I feel that research, in general, is important, because people should not waste their money, and hope on something that may not work."

No one really knows how this treatment works, what benefits to expect, or what type of individual stands to benefit. We don't even know that every person with autism has a problem with hearing. These uncertainties should make parents pause before paying a thousand dollars for a treatment their child might not need. Or, as Will Rogers said, "Why fix it, if it ain't broke?"

Are there any risks?

At this time there are no known risks to auditory training, except the possible waste of money that might be better spent on a child or his family. Some people have raised the possibility that certain individuals might become more sensitive to irritating sounds, rather than less sensitive. However, this seems unlikely, since the treatment begins with an audiogram that measures each individual's response to a spectrum of sound frequencies, and then tailors the therapy to that individual's hearing pattern.

If there is a hazard at this time, it's probably not due to Berard's suggested treatment, but the lack of control or supervision of people who act as self-employed therapists. There are virtually no standards—no license requirements, no certification system—to regulate auditory trainers at this time.

Without any kind of regulation, this field is wide open for unqualified individuals. It's easy for anyone to open a practice, and the financial incentives are very attractive. Few other fields pay ninety-five to a hundred dollars an hour after only a week's training and a small investment in equipment.

Are there any other types of sensory therapy?

Auditory training is the only therapy that uses electronic equipment to treat a sensory disorder. We simply don't have a similar way to measure and fine-tune the other four senses. There is no such thing as a "videogram" to measure sight, nor are there comparable electronic gauges for taste, smell, and touch.

Medical science has taken different directions in the diagnosis and treatment of the other sensory systems. The technological approaches are as different as the senses themselves. However, there's a common principle behind the treatment of any of these sensory disorders: identify the sensory problem and try to adjust that system so that the individual has a better chance to perceive his or her world as we perceive ours.

Are There Any Therapies for Sensory Disorders?

When we define sensory therapy in its broadest definition, we understand that there are many strategies we can consider. The drug naltrexone, mentioned in Chapter 7, is an example of medical treatment for a specific sensory disorder, an underactive sense of touch. Called an opiate-antagonist, naltrexone seems to neutralize any naturally occurring endorphins that block or reduce physical sensations. Used properly, it lets some individuals experience a more normal sense of touch, and often reduces self-injury.

Teachers and parents often discover simple ways to deal with an individual child's sensory disturbances. Generally, the quickest and easiest solution is to remove distractions or irritants from the environment; move the desk so that the student doesn't face distractions from the playground, write every instruction so that students who can't process the spoken word can read the written one, allow the child to wear his shirt inside out if he finds the inseams too uncomfortable against his skin.

There are numberless ways we can modify the school environment or relax our home rules to accommodate a child with serious sensory disorders. Imagine how other parents must change their furniture and floor plan so that a sightless child can find her way!

We should modify our homes and school rooms to help our children, but the child will probably have to adapt to the world as well. No one can strip his clothes off at work or on the bus, even if the mother sends along a permission slip, explaining that her son is tactile defensive and can't stand the feel of clothing. If your child shrieks every time someone laughs, you might work around the problem by never laughing at home, but you're not preparing her for the playground.

The parents have an ongoing challenge, deciding when they must accommodate a child with special needs, and when the child must accommodate others. Ideally, parents and teachers should discuss this openly during a child's annual Individualized Education Planning meeting.

REVIEW

Sensory disorders are responsible for most, perhaps even all, of the symptoms identified with autism. We don't have solutions for all of these sensory problems. However, occupational therapists have ways to help people adjust to oversensitivity and undersensitivity.

A treatment called auditory training may offer dramatic results, possibly even total habilitation, for hearing problems associated with autism. Though developed forty years ago in France, this therapy remained unknown in the United States until the publication of *Sound of a Miracle* in 1991. The author implied that, following ten days of treatment, her daughter began to develop normal social and academic skills and eventually overcame her autism completely.

Researchers cannot yet explain why this therapy works, or which individuals with autism are likely candidates for treatment. However, thousands of eager parents have paid for their children to take a ten-day course of treatment. Most appear satisfied with the experience, though no one has reported results as dramatic as those described in *Sound of a Miracle*.

No one has reported risks with auditory training, but very little scientific data is available yet. There are no accrediting standards for auditory trainers, so parents must make their own judgments about a therapist's qualifications.

No other treatment for sensory disorders sounds as promising as auditory training at this time. However, a medication called naltrexone appears to help some people who have undersensitivity to touch. Generally speaking, we're limited in our ability to treat sensory disorders, but we can modify our homes and learning environments so that our children can function better in spite of their sensory disorders.

Where can we get more information?

Stehli, Annabel. *Sound of a Miracle*. New York: Doubleday, 1991. This book introduced the subject of audial therapy to the public. Stehli reports a near-miraculous habilitation for her daughter after she received this therapy in Switzerland. Following the enthusiastic public response to her book, Mrs. Stehli and her husband founded a nonprofit foundation to promote auditory training worldwide. For information or to subscribe to their newsletter, write:

Georgiana Organization
P.O. Box 2607
Westport, CT 06880

The only scientific research on the subject of auditory training is being conducted at the Center for the Study of Autism, under the direction of Drs. Bernard Rimland and Stephen Edelson. For information, write or call:

Dr. Stephen Edelson
Center for the Study of Autism
Newburg, OR 97132 (503) 538-9045

11

What's a Communication Disorder?

The parent may grieve and say, "My child can't talk." However, lack of speech isn't the youngster's core problem, it's just the obvious indication of a system-wide communication disorder. You need to observe a child very carefully to determine why he doesn't speak, or what he means if he finally begins to talk.

Communication may mean many things besides speech. It can include skywriting, telegrams, pantomime, braille, even smoke signals. Technology keeps inventing new forms of communication, such as the fax machine. However, none of them will serve you unless they meet the goal of communication: to reach others with your signals—and to recognize the ones they're sending you.

A communication disorder can make you feel alone, even in a crowd. If you have ever been among people speaking with unfamiliar sounds, or tried to read a strange language, or found yourself in a gallery full of paintings you didn't understand, you've had a communication disorder. Fortunately, your disorder was temporary. You could change your situation, and be understood and understanding once again.

What's a Communication Disorder?

The student who ignores or misunderstands instructions has a communication disorder. So does the person who walks along the street talking to herself or repeating the last phrase of other speakers' comments. Regardless of speaking or writing ability, a person who can't share meanings with others has a communication disorder.

Language specialists used to call their profession speech therapy. At one time, they dealt only with the spoken word, helping students overcome speech impediments including stuttering, lisping, and problems regulating volume. Some worked with stroke patients, helping them regain lost vocabularies and language patterns. However, no one treated people with the most severe communication problems, the child who never spoke or the person who only spoke in bizarre and irrational monologues.

In the last few decades the concept of communication therapy has expanded to include much more than speech training. The profession has developed a new branch called pragmatics, dedicated to the varied uses of communication, not just the spoken forms. Therapists now address a wide variety of communication problems.

Spoken language may not be the most effective communication system for a particular person. Some people with autism learn sign language, or even keyboard writing, easier than they recognize or reproduce speech. Some use voice synthesizers, others point to pictures, either mounted on a wall chart or laminated to disks on a key chain.

Therapists try to match clients with communication systems suited to the needs and abilities of the individual. The process begins with an evaluation of a person's language comprehension (receptive language) and language usage (expressive language). Some individuals seem to have full understanding of language, but can't express it in any form. Others may reproduce all the sounds, but stay locked in repetition (echolalia) or string words and syllables together in nonsensical order (idioglossia).

What's the difference between speech, language, and communication?

The child who can't talk is a popular symbol for autism. Writers use this image because it is the simplest and most dramatic illustration of communication failure. However, silence is only one of many forms of communication disorder.

Some children with autism speak too much, or they seem to speak at the wrong time. Their communication disorder is revealed in irrelevent, even embarrassing, language. A youngster may burst into profanity in front of Grandma or recite a tampon commercial at preschool. Many families guard their language in front of a child with autism because the youngster may repeat anything or everything in the wrong place, at the wrong time.

Dr. Warren Fay, author of *Emerging Language in Autistic Children*, asks us to consider the differences between *speech*, *language*, and *communication*.

Speech refers to the spoken, or audible, use of language. It is the most obvious and mechanical of the three terms. We can tell immediately if a person is verbal, just by listening to their sounds or vocalizations. When the movements of tongue and lips produce familiar words, we call it speech. Just because words are produced, however, does not mean there is a pattern or a purpose to their use.

Parrots can imitate human sounds, but their words are only mechanical reproductions of human noise. In the same way, records and tapes speak. They reproduce our voices electronically, precisely. But the machine has no intention or judgment of its own: it's just a good sound system.

Language originally meant vocalization, but this word has come to express much more, referring to any system of signs or signals that carry meaning. *Language* implies not just sound or sight, but organization and patterns, such as grammar and syntax.

Mammals, birds, and even certain insects have language or behaviors that let them share information within their species. But the communication of animals is extremely limited. It grows out of instinct, involuntary reflexes that result in sounds or movements that send signals to others.

Computers are also said to have language, a system of recognizing and processing instructions from an operator. Computers can even "talk" to each other, in the sense that information and instructions can pass from one terminal to another.

Communication, as Dr. Fay explains, is much more complicated and varied than speech or language. *Speech* merely means the sound of language, and language depends on specific meanings for those sounds or symbols. But communication includes possibilities beyond the definitions of words. Communication uses recognition and understanding. It includes moods and shades of meaning, like humor, sarcasm, and irony.

If you return another person's smile, you communicate. If you laugh at a miming actor, or wave your hand to attract a waiter to your table, you communicate. We often communicate without using speech or language.

Communication lets us understand the messenger, as well as the message. Customs and circumstances shape the meaning as well as the words in the message. Actors say "break a leg" to other performers, because that's a traditional way to say "good luck" in the theater. When people greet us with "How are you?" it's not a question about our health. We're expected to say, "Fine, thanks, and you?"

By the time people grow up in a culture, they understand that words mean different things in different situations. We don't speak the same way to strangers, co-workers, and family members. We know when it's acceptable to joke at dinner, and when it isn't in church. We learn to interpret remarks from other people and to shape our communication according to relationships. Sometimes tone of voice, posture, and expression are more important than the words we use.

What causes communication disorders?

It takes a complicated network of nerves and brain cells to manage the human communication system. Signals and sensations have to move through the sensory organs to parts of the brain that process language. After a series of connections and judgments, signals travel back out to the body parts that produce sound and gesture.

Whenever a part of this system fails, it causes a communication disorder. The problem may be with the "receptive language" process (receiving messages through sound, image, etc.) or with "expressive language" (expressing through speech, gesture, or other motor activity). Most people with autism have both receptive and expressive language problems.

We don't have the technology to "troubleshoot" a person's communication circuits. We can't detect a faulty neurological connection until we see the resulting developmental delay. Neurological problems are often the *why* behind the communication disorder, but technology has yet to show us the precise connection between the brain cells (which we can't see) and the final, noticeable behaviors.

Obviously, people with communication disorders can't explain their disability to us. Therapists even find it hard to tell what a patient *can* and *cannot* do. Evaluation, then, has to begin with observation. We must ask, "What does this child *do* that's different?" or "What *doesn't* this child do that the average child his age does?"

Common problems in autism include poor eye contact, unusual reactions to sound, and the avoidance of people. These symptoms leave us wondering, "What's wrong with his vision?" "How does she hear things?" "Does touch bother this child?" Sensory problems can distort the message a child gets from his eyes and ears. The message becomes more distorted when language is involved. The listener has to pass the message not only through the ears, but through the brain cells that recognize and process language.

Speech pathologists are making remarkable discoveries about the brain's organization of language. Stroke patients often have speech loss called aphasia. Lesions in the brain result in damage that blocks the recall of certain words. Sometimes the damage is so minor that patients forget only one of a word's many uses. It may block only the written or spoken form of a word, but not both. In fact, some patients will forget only the verb form, or the noun form, of a word like *paint*. Apparently, the brain stores the word in four different areas of memory or even in four different ways: a written and an oral form of the verb (to paint the house) and a written and an oral form of the noun (a bucket of paint).

Every time the patient stumbles on one of these four uses, it shows miniscule damage to the brain's language system. And yet the brain is only a single part of our communication equipment. We use neuromotor systems to operate the mouth and body parts, for example, to shape the lips or to nod "yes" to a request.

Why don't some people talk?

Delay or failure to speak is certainly the most noticeable sign of a communication disorder. This doesn't necessarily mean that every nonverbal child has the same problem. The parent may grieve and say, "My child can't talk." However, lack of speech isn't the youngster's core problem, it's just the obvious indication of a system-wide communication disorder. You need to observe a child very carefully to determine why he or she doesn't speak. Possibilities include:

A) Problems hearing or recognizing sounds
B) Inability to remember sounds or associate words
C) Problems producing sounds or gestures

Most professionals will test a child's hearing as a first step. However, a hearing test doesn't always pick up problems of recognizing separate sounds. The child usually needs an evaluation of receptive language to see how well he or she can understand and follow requests. If the youngster scores well in hearing and receptive language, the problem may simply be language expression. Expressive language problems don't necessarily mean the person doesn't comprehend. Perhaps he understands speech and even writing, but can't master the fine motor control required to speak or write. Professionals call this disability apraxia, meaning "unable to practice," as we will see in the next chapter on facilitated communication.

Do verbal people have communication disorders?

Absolutely! It's important to remember that verbalization is not the same as communication. Most people with autism are verbal, but their language habits can show severe developmental problems.

Communication therapists look at how people use language: Does your child use words to identify objects? To request them? Is speech used in the right circumstances, or is it always delayed and repetitive? Can the child use pronouns correctly, calling himself "I" or "me" and saying "you" when speaking to another?

It's important to examine how a speaker uses words. She should choose verbs to accurately reflect time and quantity. Does she know the difference between *eat* and *ate*? Does she match the verb to subjects, saying "Suzy *is*," and "girls *are*," or "he *does*" and "they *do?*"

A few ungrammatical verbs don't prove a person has a communication disorder, but frequent misuse of tenses and plurals should lead you to take a closer look at the person's language pattern. Maybe he can't use *before* or *after* correctly because he doesn't understand time. Maybe he never says *enough* or *too much* because he doesn't understand *less* and *more*, expressions of quantity.

Some people understand "concrete words," names for things they can see or touch, but don't grasp "abstract words," the language of ideas. They might use *water*, and *stove* correctly, but can't express concepts such as *liquid* or *heat*. Names of specific, visible objects are the easiest to master. When a word expresses generalities or qualities, it becomes harder for some people to understand. *Coat* is a concrete word, *clothing* refers to garments in general, and *fashion* suggests a quality that some, but not all, coats may have.

We rely on abstract language to communicate about the past and the future, using words to let us "see" and describe things we can never point to; things that no longer exist, are yet to come, or may never be. Without language, communication stays frozen in the "here and now." You can't point to time and space.

What forms can communication disorders take?

As Chapter 4 explains, autism affects people in different ways, but there is always some communication disorder. Most people have both receptive and expressive language delays, but the degree is often hard to recognize.

Some children show typical language development until the age of eighteen to twenty months. The child babbles during infancy and follows a typical developmental schedule, using single words around the first birthday and short phrases within six more months. Then the language suddenly stops before age two. Some children continue making vocal sounds and seem to think they are talking. Others are nearly silent. Occasionally, children surprise their parents with a few sudden words. They may speak once, but never again.

A few children with autism learn language years after others have given up hope. It's often assumed that if a child doesn't speak by the age of four or five, she probably never will. But some learn even later. A few can recall their earlier, nonverbal phase and can even talk about it. For example, a woman we'll call Connie recalls the day she discovered speech.

When Connie was three years old and totally nonverbal, her parents enrolled her in a therapeutic preschool. Like many children with autism, Connie had no trouble learning the shapes of letters and the order of the alphabet. Teachers taught her to read and to copy words. She became literate by the age of six, yet never spoke.

"I could hear people," Connie remembers. "I knew they made sounds with their faces, but I never paid attention." The sounds of speech meant no more to her than the noise of traffic or running water. Then, "One day the teacher was helping me at the blackboard, and I suddenly knew there was a connection between the words we were writing and the sounds she was making!"

A new world opened for Connie, not the world of sound, for she had always heard noises. She had discovered something the rest of us take for granted; *vocal sounds have meaning!* Connie's insight at the blackboard sounds like the scene in *The Miracle Worker* when the blind, deaf Helen Keller discovered that her teacher's finger movements had meaning, a meaning that would teach her to communicate.

After her moment of insight, Connie began to pay attention to voices for the first time. Eventually, she learned to listen and to talk as well as she could read and write. In technical language, we would say that she suffered from "verbal agnosia," an inability to recognize language. Her reading skills became a bridge that taught her to understand the spoken word. She's verbal now, but still has massive gaps in understanding.

To some extent, we can identify with Connie and others who experience agnosia. When we find ourselves around people speaking a language we've never heard, we can't recognize or remember the specific sounds. However, we already know about language (our own), so we listen. We pay attention until we hear patterns in the foreign tongue.

What's a Communication Disorder?

We expect the "sounds people make with their faces" to have meaning, because we learned that in our infancy. Some people with autism don't have that advantage.

Verbal agnosia may be the most serious learning disability connected with autism. Every announcement, each instruction—every spoken word—would sound meaningless and random to a person with verbal agnosia. That person couldn't be a "listener," for words wouldn't seem meaningful enough to hold his interest.

People who recognize and understand language may still have serious communication disorders related to problems of expressive language, as opposed to receptive language. Some individuals can't control their speech output, in spite of normal hearing that lets them imitate words perfectly. Their thoughts may suit the occasion, but their words don't. Baffling or inappropriate phrases fly out of their mouths: "She was hotter than a two-dollar pistol," spoken to the grocery clerk, or "Would you like a fat lip?" to the mail carrier. A child may greet his teacher saying, "Horses are made out of Kool-Aid," instead of, "Hi, how are you?"

Books on autism use the term *echolalia* to describe one pattern of language disturbance. For reasons we don't fully understand, some people can only repeat or "echo" phrases they've heard others use. It makes it difficult for them to answer simple questions. If a parent asks, "Do you want juice or milk?" the child may say, "Want juice or milk."

Echolalia is usually an instant replay of words used by another person or heard on radio or television. However, some people also demonstrate longer term memory with "delayed echolalia." Sometimes a person with autism will quote speech fragments heard days, or even years, earlier.

Listeners find it puzzling when a child quotes a weather report, a song, or a commercial for no apparent reason, leaving us to wonder, "Why did he say that now? Is there an association between what the child really wants to say, and the words that tumbled out? What's the connection?"

Generally speaking, echolalia isn't functional speech. It doesn't communicate intent to the listener. However, Dr.

Fay and many communication therapists think echolalia is a promising sign of potential communication.

An echolalic speaker often pronounces words well and has good language memory. Sometimes parents or teachers recognize patterns in a child's echolalia. "Want some juice?" might be a standard phrase a child uses to ask for a snack. Perhaps the child can't request specific items but uses the echolalic phrase every time she's thirsty or hungry. In other words, though the child doesn't use the phrase or sentence according to its exact meaning, she has made an appropriate association between those words and the thought she'd really like to express.

Echolalia shows that speakers either don't understand or can't apply the rules of communication. They can't access their own vocabularly to select the right words and connect them to form an original message. They can't tailor statements to fit new situations. In a roundabout adaptation to this, they repeat known phrases, hoping that one will communicate their intention or desire.

People with echolalic language sometimes make meaningless and bizarre sounds called idioglossia. The term means "language of idiots," or speech without reason. The speaker may have some purpose in mind, but the speech makes no sense to a listener.

Idioglossia may include real words in nonsensical patterns ("baby hippo meatballs"), or just a string of vocal sounds ("adda, babba, buzzy, wuzzy, wuzzy"). Some children have favorite sayings they repeat often. Perhaps they like the rhythm or sounds of their babbling. Maybe they enjoy the vibration of tongue against lips or palate. The communication disorder can hide many secrets.

Many children outgrow obvious echolalia and idioglossia. In fact, some with mild forms of autism never show these patterns of speech. However, a careful evaluation of their expressive language usually shows limits or failure of communication. Sometimes minor problems, such as confusion with verbs or pronouns, cause misunderstandings.

People with even mild forms of autism often find communication painful and frustrating.

We need to listen carefully in order to recognize a child's specific communication problems. Try to identify the individual's language pattern. This will let you understand the person better and will help you in your search for appropriate solutions. You'll be able to choose activities that let the youngster practice more purposeful communication.

What's the connection between communication and behavior?

Early books on autism listed communication difficulties and behavior problems as if they were separate symptoms. However, psychologists and communication specialists now recognize that the behaviors of people with autism are closely tied to their communication disorders.

Generally, people with autism have problems with the nonverbal aspects of communication, including eye contact and body language. They may not be able to interpret other people's tone of voice, facial expression, or posture. They may interrupt others, because they can't judge the pace of a conversation or wait their turn to speak.

Dr. Margaret Creedon has found that children with autism cannot follow moving objects with their eyes as fast as the typical child. When a teacher points to an image on the blackboard or a mother says, "Look at the doggie," most children have eye movements that appear immediate or spontaneous. A delay in eye movements can disrupt the connection between image and verbal command, making it harder for the learner to "see" what the teacher is trying to teach.

Creedon's research supports Dr. Eric Courchesne's claim that people with autism have biologically based problems with focus and attention. This makes it hard, if not impossible, to process many of the subtler gestures (the wink of an eye, curl of the lips, or furrow of the brow) in another person's communication. Simply put, people with autism have trouble recognizing other peoples' attitudes—and attitude is often the most important part of a message, conveying sincerity, sympathy, sarcasm, or even ridicule.

When the communication system fails, some people quit trying. Sometimes children discover that it's easier to grab what they want than to struggle with words. People with limited language often discover that temper tantrums bring them quicker results than an attempt to negotiate verbally. Tragically, many decide that violent behaviors are more effective than the words we try so hard to teach them.

Once aggressive or bizarre behavior becomes a habit, it's hard to change. This dynamic is also at work when poor communication fosters violence and self-abuse, behaviors parents can't ignore. Too often, the response to those behaviors encourages repetition. Some children with autism develop behavior patterns that become more of a problem than their original disability.

Fortunately, there is a way to break a cycle of negative behavior. Psychologists can apply a process called functional analysis of behavior, a technique that begins with the belief that human behavior has meaning.

People do things for a reason, though others may not recognize the individual's intent. However, if we observe someone's behavior long enough, we can usually find a pattern, an association with events or circumstances. Finding that pattern helps us discover the purpose behind a behavior. You may have to take several guesses before you understand why a person behaves in an unusual or irrational manner.

The behaviors classified as self-abuse, or SIBs (self-injurious behaviors), are particularly hard to understand. Why would a person bite his wrist or arm until it bleeds? What would make a child pinch his own flesh until it's bruised or broken? It could be an effective way to attract attention, a craving for topical sensory stimulation, or a random act of frustration. You may have to follow several different hunches before you find one that leads to understanding and solution.

One of the best books written on functional analysis of behavior is *Progress Without Punishment*, by Dr. Anne Donnellan. This book maps out techniques for first observing, then analyzing problem behaviors. Donnellan and her circle of colleagues, including Drs. Gary LaVigna and Marcia Datlow Smith, have amazing rates of success solving behavior problems with severly disabled people.

How can you teach communication?

The field of communication therapy has more to offer people with autism at present than any other profession. Therapists look for patterns in the child's verbal and nonverbal behavior. Then, they teach the child a communication system that matches his or her own abilities.

Some children can't master every form of communication. Sensory disabilities can interfere with speech or writing. Neuromotor problems may stifle the child, or mental deficits limit his or her understanding of language. However, all children can practice the social functions of communication. Each child needs to request, refuse, and negotiate.

Communication therapists who understand autism focus on the functions of language more than the form. They don't make nonverbal children copy language sounds, an exercise as useless as repairing the turn signal on a car that has no steering wheel. The specialist knows that meaningful communication is driven by function, not form.

The average child follows a predictable path toward communication. The first steps don't even involve words. For example, children begin with "motoral communication" before they master symbol or gesture. In this first phase of communication, they recognize the usefulness of bigger people. They may grab parents by the hand and lead them in the direction of desired objects. This is the most primitive and limited form of communication. The other person isn't seen as a "listener," but, merely as an object that can help the child. Yet this is a start toward socialization.

After a stage of motoral communication, children usually discover gesture. They find they can attract our attention by pointing or waving. Those gestures are faster and more versatile than motorally directing another person. Pointing to a door has several possible meanings: I want to go, I want you to leave, or I want Daddy to come home. Some children develop quite a gestural vocabulary. They may use smiles and body language, besides hand gestures, to communicate greetings and requests, and for play.

Peekaboo makes a great activity during the gestural phase. Adult and child take turns hiding their eyes, making eye contact, and acting surprised. This teaches fundamental rules for later communication, rules like: make sure you get the other person's attention; use gestures he understands; and respond to others as they respond to you. The game works with or without words.

Research has shown that parents are the first to recognize a communication disturbance in a child. More often than not, a mother or father will recognize the problem before the pediatrician. If you notice that your child isn't pointing or using single words by twelve to eighteen months, watch closely. If she doesn't start chaining two or three words together by the age of two, it's time to take a good look at a pediatrician's developmental calendar. Your child may need a professional evaluation.

Either a communication therapist or a developmental psychologist can do the evaluation. They check hearing and vision, then observe behaviors tied to the child's needs and interests. Chances are even a severely disabled child shows some form of communicative behavior. Perhaps the youngster merely shrieks or cries. The therapist looks for variations in the behavior and possible meanings behind it.

Dr. Diane Twachtman, an education consultant in Glastonbury, Connecticut, believes in an environmental approach to communication training. She suggests rearranging furnishings, both at home and in the classroom, so that the child has more need to communicate.

Some children find it easier to help themselves than to ask the mother or teacher for help. The more children can do alone, the less they need to communicate. Twachtman recommends placing favorite toys and food on a shelf out of the child's reach. Eventually, the child has to take an adult to the shelf (a form of motoral communication) or at least point to the object (gestural communication).

An environmental approach to communication training relies on a few rules:

A) Create a need to communicate. This motivates the child to interact with others.

B) Don't make the challenge too difficult, or the child will give up. Accept whatever form of communication the child shows competence in.

C) When the child makes a reasonable effort to communicate, reward him. It's important to let the child find success through communication, whether the form is motoral, gestural, verbal, or otherwise.

D) Create choice-making opportunities for the child and make her indicate her choice. Don't make choices for her or anticipate her preference. Play dumb, if necessary, so the child has to show you or tell you what she wants.

E) Periodically look at the child's progress to set new goals. Goals should challenge the child to use his present skills in more circumstances or move on to experiment with a new communication form (perhaps speech, signing, or writing).

F) Make sure the child finds his communication efforts successful. Communicative behaviors need recognition and reward, both at school and at home. If the teacher ignores a gesture, or the parent does everything for the child, it hampers learning. The child needs confidence that his gesture or language will work, not just in one setting, but out in the world.

Parents and teachers share the responsibility for communication therapy. In fact, everyone in the child's environment plays a part in this training. If a bus driver, a lunchroom attendant, or a grandparent ignores the child's efforts at communication, the child loses confidence and may not try again.

Whenever someone rewards negative communication— screams, tantrums, or abuse—it gives the wrong message to the child. People with autism rely on us to show them acceptable ways to communicate. If we pay more attention to the negative than the positive, we teach a dangerous lesson: "When communication fails, try violence," or "grabbing is easy, so why bother asking?"

REVIEW

Communication disorders refer to distortions, misunderstandings, or barriers that block the sharing of meaning between individuals. People who can't hear, see, or read have trouble receiving messages, a *receptive* language problem. Those who can't speak, gesture, or write, have an *expressive* communication disorder.

Everyone with autism has some problems with receptive or expressive language, or both. The most obvious, and first diagnosed, are children who are nonverbal. Yet verbal people may have problems that are just as serious. Some are able to repeat words but can't use language in a meaningful way.

Fortunately, there are alternatives to the spoken word. Some people do better with another system, such as writing, signing or gesture. We need to help people find a form that works for them. Those who can't hear a message may be able to read it. If the eyes don't work, the fingers may master braille. If symbols and letters make no sense to a person, perhaps a picture or sign language will.

A typical child goes through communication stages, from motoral, to gestural, to verbal. Most people with autism go through the same steps, only much more slowly. Some won't make it beyond certain stages.

Communication therapy encourages interaction between the individual and others. It begins with a search for behaviors that have a common meaning to both parties. If the child doesn't learn positive communicative behaviors, he or she may discover negative ones. Maladaptive and antisocial behaviors suggest the individual is trying to interact, but can't do it with language.

What else should I read?

Donnellan, Anne. *Progress Without Punishment: Effective Approaches for Learners with Behavior Problems*. New York: Teachers College Press, 1988.

Fay, Warren. *Emerging Language in Autistic Children*. Baltimore: University Park Press, 1980.

12

What Is Facilitated Communication?

You can forget hope
it's easy
But only hope will set you free.

—David Eastham

David Eastham understood hope better than most poets. Before his death by drowning, he left a collection of poems about his yearnings and feelings. Those are common topics in poetry, but people who believed the stereotypes thought David couldn't understand those subjects, because he had autism.

Since the first research in 1943, we have always questioned how autism affects mood and understanding. People with autism don't express emotions in a typical way, so others thought they had fewer feelings. Some professionals even claimed that people with autism couldn't love or develop bonds with other people.

David lived his short life in the shadow of autism. He was fortunate, though, in that he had a mother with enough patience and ingenuity to enable him to overcome his communication disability. Mrs. Eastham tutored her son at home. She knew he couldn't learn through standard means, so she taught him the shapes of letters through touch. Using sandpaper and smooth plastic letters, she trained him to recognize shapes and signs with his fingertips. He seemed able to process tactile stimulation, though sounds and print had failed to reach him.

The boy learned to associate letters with speech and written words. By the age of fourteen, he could read. Then, there was no stopping him. David never spoke, but he learned to type and quickly went beyond simple requests and "yes" or "no" responses. Before long, he was writing poetry and studying at the college level. His success astounded even his mother.

David was never "cured" of autism. He continued to show symptoms of the disability until his death, but he had the mind and literary talent of a poet.

Mrs. Eastham hasn't received the credit she deserves. People thought her son's success was just another one-of-a-kind fluke connected with autism, but David's writing demonstrated more than an ability to type. It proved that, behind the verbal apraxia, he had normal intelligence and emotions, *things people with autism weren't supposed to have!*

The Easthams' achievement showed that nonverbal people aren't always as limited as we believe. Yet this family's experience was not unique. Other families would make the discovery again and again before the world would pay attention. One of the first pioneers was a mother in California, Aurelia Schawlow.

Aurelia Schawlow's discovery began in 1981 when she went to Stockholm to see her husband accept a Nobel prize in physics. In Scandinavia, she heard about a mother who had taught her autistic son to communicate with a keyboard. Back home, Mrs. Schawlow spent two years trying the same technique with her twenty-five-year-old son. He finally responded on a hand-held device called a Canon Communicator.

His first words weren't remarkable. When his mother asked Arthur Schawlow, Jr., "What would you like to do?"

He typed, "PIZZA." She eagerly rewarded him with a trip to a pizza parlor.

After he finished eating, she asked, "Now, what would you like to do?"

"MCDONALD'S." They got back in the car and drove to the nearest McDonald's, where he ate again. Then she asked once more, "What would you like to do next, Artie?"

"SIZZLER."

Mrs. Schawlow agreed to a final food reward. But when he had finished his third meal, she said, "'We're not going to any more restaurants today, Artie. Tell me someplace else you'd like to go."

"HOME."

"Do you want me to take you back to your home?" (Artie was living in a mental hospital at the time.)

"NO . . . YOUR HOME."

The Schawlows arranged to keep Artie at home for a few days. Aurelia continued working with her son, gently supporting his hand over the keyboard of the Canon Communicator. In this position he could press a key with minimal effort by merely straightening his finger or poking. This would print a letter on a strip of paper.

Before long, the conversations between mother and son grew more complicated. Artie told Aurelia he had learned to read seventeen years earlier at the age of ten, but had never been able to show anyone. He had grown up unable to indicate simple choices or to express his personality and his opinion.

She asked him if he would like to visit a young man with Down syndrome and his mother. Artie answered, "NO."

"Why?" she asked.

"BECAUSE SHE'S SILLY AND HE'S STUPID!"

Aurelia was surprised to read those words. She didn't use those terms to describe people. Besides, *silly* and *stupid* aren't factual expressions; they show personal judgment. People with autism weren't supposed to be capable of judgment or judgmental language.

In 1985 Dr. and Mrs. Schawlow spoke at the annual conference of the Autism Society of America. They told an audience of several hundred people about their son's progress. By that time, Aurelia and her son could carry on full conversations with no apparent limits to Artie's understanding or vocabulary. She no longer had to suspend his hand above the Canon Communicator. He still depended upon her touch for encouragement, but she decreased the amount of support. Sometimes she only grasped his elbow while he ran his fingers across the keyboard.

She knew there were doubters. Some professionals had already called Artie's messages "the Ouija board effect." They thought that wishful thinking led her to guide his finger to letters of her unconscious choice. The Schawlows thought an audience of other parents, other people who might want to experiment, would believe them.

Many people congratulated the Schawlows, but few seemed interested in trying the technique. Artie Schawlow's achievement, like David Eastham's, seemed another one-of-a-kind fluke. For years authorities on autism had used a pat answer for achievements they couldn't understand: "Everyone with autism is different." This half-truth kept them from exploring a trail the Schawlows had already blazed.

Meanwhile, Carol Lee Berger, a communication disorder specialist in Eugene, Oregon, began experimenting with her students at a computer keyboard. She positioned a child in a chair in front of the computer and sat behind him, taking his hand so that she could point his finger to the keyboard. Inadvertently, she stumbled across a technique being tried by another teacher on the other side of the world.

In Australia, a therapist named Rosemary Crossley was trying a nearly identical technique with people who had cerebral palsy. Crossley found that she could help many of them communicate by supporting their hand or arm to reduce the amount of involuntary jerking. After several successful years of practice, she decided to try the approach on someone with autism.

Crossley chose a seven-year-old who appeared severely disabled. He wasn't toilet trained, never made eye contact, and grabbed anything he wanted. He had a pattern of aggressive behavior, including fits, vomiting, scratching, and running away.

Rosemary held the child on her lap and showed him a voice synthesizer, then a Canon Communicator. Supporting his wrist over the keyboard, she demonstrated how to print letters on the paper strip. She typed his name, "JONATHAN." To her surprise, then he typed JONOTHAN." She later checked with the child's mother and found the boy had been right. In his first communication session, he had corrected his teacher's spelling!

Before long, Crossley and her colleagues at Dignity through Education and Language Communication Centre in Melbourne, Australia, began practicing the technique with more children and adults with autism. They considered themselves facilitators for the person with the communication disorder and named their approach facilitated communication.

News of Crossley's work reached Dr. Douglas Biklen at Syracuse University in New York. Biklen's first reaction was disbelief. In the *Harvard Educational Review* ("*Communication Unbound: Autism and Praxis*" August 1990) he wrote:

I had been shocked by a letter from Australia that described Crossley's success in using a new technique to allow people with autism to communicate. The letter claimed that Crossley was eliciting "high-level" communication from her students. "Sophisticated written (typed) communication at sentence level," I was told. I didn't know what to think about this claim. It seemed conceivable to me that Crossley and her colleagues had happened on a *few* people with autism for whom such communication was possible. But it made no sense that people who had been classified as severely intellectually disabled would have normal or even near-normal literacy skills. By definition, people with autism who do not speak or who speak only a small range of phrases are referred to as "low-functioning" and are thought to have a severe intellectual disability as well.

Biklen had to travel to Australia to see Crossley's program for himself. What he saw convinced him that Rosemary had not "happened on a few people with autism for whom such communication was possible." In Australia he saw the technique work with numerous people, who impressed him with a range of thoughts and emotions he had never suspected people with autism could express.

In her clinic, Rosemary Crossley trained student after student, whereas Mrs. Eastham and Mrs. Schawlow had only one pupil apiece. A few parents had known that simple motor problems, a failure of coordination, could hide normal understanding, but Crossley and Biklen brought this to the world's attention.

Has facilitated communication changed our understanding of autism?

Doug Biklen's comments in the *Harvard Educational Review* made a tremendous impact on the field of autism. Professionals around the world were surprised to read that the communication problem might not indicate lack of understanding, but a failure of the neuromotor system, an inability to practice language because the vocal system and writing hand couldn't perform without assistance or "facilitation."

Some professionals had heard this before as isolated reports from parents, but this time it wasn't wishful thinking from a doting mother. Another professional had made the idea acceptable by publishing in a famous educational journal.

Facilitated communication raises new issues and challenges old assumptions: Is autism merely a neuromotor failure, or praxis? Will facilitated communication work for everyone? Does every nonverbal person who has been dependent on sign language or gestural communication have higher thinking ability which they can show through facilitated communication?

We don't have the answers yet, but these questions have overturned so many professional beliefs and practices that the dust still hasn't settled. Psychologists, educators, and communication specialists are eager to evaluate facilitated communication, and some are convinced it will change the way they serve people. Others think it's a fad, or even a hoax (the Ouija board effect). Many consider facilitated communication a useful discovery, but think some claims raise unrealistic expectations. No one knows how many people will benefit or how much their lives will really change.

It will take time and carefully evaluated studies to judge the potential of facilitated communication. Meanwhile, thousands of people want to try the technique *now* on a child or student. Many parents believe facilitated communication is their first and best hope for understanding a child with autism.

Biklen and his associates schedule frequent workshops in Syracuse, New York, and the Boston-based Adriana Foundation has toured the country offering information and individual assessments. A new profession has even sprung up, the trained "facilitator." This person evaluates prospective students and trains parents and teachers to act as facilitators.

Within a year after the article in the *Harvard Educational Review*, network television interviewed Biklen. The program suggested that *most* people with autism could benefit from facilitated communication, and Biklen mentioned that the technique may even help people with autism who, though verbal, have limited or nonsensical use of language. He claims that some individuals use better grammar on the keyboard than during speech. Facilitated communication lets them communicate at a higher level than their teachers and parents would have predicted.

A number of experts think it's too early to praise facilitated communication unequivocally. Many are waiting to see more research. Scientific investigation, however, moves very slowly, especially when it has to go against the tide of established authority. Yet there is a growing demand for legal proof.

In *Annie's Coming Out* (New York: Penquin, 1980) Rosemary Crossley tells about going to court to prove that a client with cerebral palsy had control of messages made through facilitated communication. The facilitator (Crossley) left the courtroom so that she couldn't hear messages others would ask the client to transmit to Crossley. Crossley returned to the room and facilitated the client with the keyboard. Correct responses convinced the Supreme Court of Victoria that the client, not the facilitator, had control of the communication.

Similar court cases are pending in the United States. Several communication facilitators claim that a client with autism has charged third parties with physical or sexual abuse. When those cases go before a judge, facilitated communication, as well as the defendant, will go on trial. Attorneys will have to prove or disprove the validity of testimony offered through a facilitator, instead of by direct cross-examination.

How does facilitated communication work?

This technique begins with a trusting, accepting relationship between the facilitator and the student. Mrs. Schawlow and Mrs. Eastham followed their motherly instincts. They forced nothing on their sons, but patiently repeated the opportunity to learn.

Biklen and Crossley have both written articles that tell how to introduce an individual to facilitated communication. They offer some very sensible advice in copyrighted material. Anyone interested in trying this without guidance from an experienced facilitator should read the publications from Syracuse University or DEAL (Dignity through Education And Language).

Most facilitators recommend using the Canon Communicator instead of another keyboard. The Canon has a simple alphabetical keyboard. A light touch on a key makes the communicator print the letter on a strip of paper.

First, the facilitator needs to determine whether the student prefers to use the left or the right hand. Next, it's necessary to find out how well the person understands the alphabet. Can he or she touch a y to indicate "yes" and an n to say "no"? Will the learner touch the first letter of other familiar words to make choices or to answer questions?

The facilitator needs to experiment to find out how much support an individual student needs. Some learners catch on quickly and only need help bearing the weight of their writing hand. Others make much slower progress. Sometimes the facilitator has to suspend the student's hand slightly above the surface of the keyboard. This lets the student touch a key with an absolute minimum of physical effort.

Experienced facilitators recommend starting with simple, nonthreatening questions. Don't ask a beginning student, "Why don't you talk?" or "What do you want to do with your life?" Keep the lessons simple until the learner shows the ability and the willingness to go on to more difficult or personal discussions.

Facilitated communication is more likely to work if the facilitator follows the rules of general communication training:

> A) Let the student make the choices.
> B) Reward the learner for each successful communication.
> C) Never force a task if the student isn't ready.

Keep the activity challenging and interesting for the learner. Ideally, you want the individual to take more and more responsibility for the communication. So the facilitator should try to reduce or "fade" support as quickly as possible. As the facilitator, move your hand from a beginning position supporting the student's palm and index finger, back to the wrist, the elbow, or even the shoulder. Fading the facilitator's support encourages the students to exert more effort on their own, possibly developing independent use of the communicator. Fading the support also reassures the facilitator that the student has taken charge of her own messages.

Involve other facilitators as early as possible. If the learner becomes dependent on a single facilitator, it limits communication to times when that person is available to help. Alternative facilitators encourage the student to communicate in more situations. Artie Schawlow enjoyed fluent communication with his mother, but he never worked with other facilitators. When she died in 1991, Artie quit using his Canon Communicator. His confidence seemed to die with her.

If possible, the student should work with more than one facilitator for other reasons, too. A single facilitator, either mother, father, or teacher, may feel pressured to produce a meaningful message. The interpersonal relationship between child and facilitator can introduce factors that distract from the actual communicative purpose of the exercise.

Some facilitators think they have to elicit a meaningful message every time they assist an individual with autism. They may reason, "If I'm a paid facilitator, I have to come up with some evidence that this technique works." Or, "If I'm a good mother, my child should respond to my supportive touch."

People who have severe disabilities and limited personal contacts generally wish to please their caregivers, so they feel pressure to perform as well as their facilitator. This personal interaction between an anxious facilitator and an emotionally dependent student may distract from the fundamental purpose of facilitated communication, which is to help the disabled persons express their own thoughts.

It's not always clear to observers, or even to facilitators themselves, whether a client has deliberately chosen to push a key. Often, a trembling finger is redirected to

touch a neighboring key. A pulse beat may be misinter-
preted as voluntary movement. Facilitators take the responsibility for deciding whether a finger's action is
intentional or spasmodic.

Using more than one facilitator helps prove the validity
of communication. The student's messages should reflect
her or his own language and personality, not the facilitators'. If an individual types different messages depending
on the facilitator, it suggests that the facilitator, not the
student, has shaped the communication.

In February, 1992, many people were shocked to read
about a landmark case in Australia that ruled against the
testimony of Rosemary Crossley and her colleagues. In this
case, a young woman with severe disabilities had been removed from her family home and her family members ac-
cused of aggravated sexual abuse.

As in the earlier case that tested the ability of a woman
with cerebral palsy to communicate with the aid of a facilitator, the courtroom became a stage, not just for an individual's testimony, but for arguments pro and con about
facilitated communication.

News of this case traveled quickly around the world, fuel-
ing the skepticism of those who had already opposed the
idea of facilitated communication. The circumstances discussed in court suggest that a few impressionable facilitators had been too zealous, and libelously inaccurate, in
their interpretation of incomplete words and messages produced during sessions with their client. After those un-
happy allegations had been disproved, the court returned
the client to her family.

Defense witnesses, Drs. Robert Cummings and Margot
Prior, challenged that facilitated communication "fosters an
apparent cult of deception and illusion." A reporter covering the trial observed: "Throughout the two-week hearing,
the intellectually disabled woman attended with most of
her family. Although clearly unaware of the technicalities,
she displayed her joy and love for her family and sensitivity
to the highly charged emotions in the room."

This court verdict doesn't show that facilitated communication is a fraud, or that people with autism can't express themselves through this system. It merely points out the hazards of zealous facilitators, jumping to conclusions based upon their own social attitudes or assumptions. It warns us that we must be sensitive to the limitations, as well as the personality, of the client. It could prove destructive to offer "too much" assistance to learners who miss keys or seem to falter in their spelling or grammar.

Some parents are afraid to try facilitated communication without help from an experienced facilitator. This fear makes sense. We still don't understand the neurological reasons behind verbal apraxia. However, experienced facilitators insist that their own confidence and positive attitude play an important role in helping the challenged individual explore facilitated communication. An experienced facilitator might have more success with the first lesson than a nervous parent.

Does facilitated communication work for everyone?

The world paid little attention to David Eastham's poetry or Artie Schawlow's use of the Communicator. People either doubted their skills or thought they were "one-of-a-kind" case studies. Doug Biklen was only one of many skeptics who thought that Crossley had chanced upon a few people who could respond to facilitated communication.

From his first correspondence with Crossley to his later appearance on national television, Biklen changed his mind about facilitated communication. He's been quoted as saying that 90 percent of the people with autism may benefit from this technique. We are still waiting for well-controlled studies to sort out fact from wishful thinking. How many people have apraxia that could be overcome through facilitated communication? The answer probably lies somewhere between Biklen's first skepticism ("a few individuals") and his later, more optimistic, projections (90 percent).

Chapter 4 explains that autism doesn't affect all individuals in the same way. There appear to be many developmental patterns, each caused by damage to different neurological pathways. It's very unlikely that any one treatment or therapy will work with 90 percent of such a varied population.

According to their mothers, both David Eastham and Artie Schawlow had normally developing speech until the toddler stage. Other parents have described what it's like to watch an apparently normal child lose speech and gesture. It seems that some children have a progressive form of apraxia that destroys verbal communication. Perhaps they represent a subtype that has no intellectual limits, merely neuromotor interference with speech. They may have the intellectual capacity to think, emote, and communicate, but can't perform the physical movements (of mouth, lips, and tongue) necessary to speak.

Some parents report that a nonverbal child speaks on unpredictable occasions. Many others notice that a verbal child communicates differently under stress. Some speak better, others lose verbal control. The experiences of these different families suggest there are many kinds of selective damage to the speech system. Apraxia may be a feature of most forms of communication disorder, but it doesn't account for all of the other related communication problems a child may have.

Has facilitated communication really changed our understanding of autism? Biklen says yes, but it depends on our original understanding. People who thought poor verbal skill meant low intelligence need to take another look. Yet others knew that autism covered a baffling variety of symptoms and talents. They find it easy to believe that verbal apraxia may hide normal intelligence.

Facilitated communication doesn't disprove all of the earlier research on autism. It merely shows that we underestimated the variety of developmental patterns. We need to find out who can benefit from this technique. Then we'll know more about the different patterns within the broader diagnosis of autism.

Can facilitated communication make an important change in my child's life?

As with any other treatment, you must consider facilitated communication within the broad context of your child's autism, his or her particular abilities and problems, history, and personality. Facilitated communication is not a cure-all, though public reaction has been overwhelming. Some people, however, expect too much, perhaps because they misunderstand autism. Speech or writing has never been the only challenge facing people with autism. Many of these individuals also have obsessive–compulsive disorders, seizure patterns, and social problems beyond the scope of language.

Facilitated communication won't overcome all of the individual's neurological problems, and the people who master this technique still face many challenges in day-to-day living. Then, there are others who will never learn this skill.

Some people may learn to use the keyboard without a facilitator. David Eastham did, and he was able to make astounding progress academically and socially before he drowned. Others may always remain like Artie Schawlow, dependent on a single, trusted facilitator to make their voices heard.

At the very least, facilitated communication has taught us to respect nonverbal people more. Before this, many thought intelligence depended on verbal ability. Even professionals who should have known better made this mistake. Some teachers didn't teach reading to nonverbal children because they thought the children couldn't possibly learn. More children will get the benefit of the doubt from now on.

Research will probably show wide variations in individuals' ability to use facilitated communication. Some people may master high-functioning communication, expressing choices and negotiating changes in their school, work, and residential programs. But others may never become fluent with the keyboard. Some people with echolalic speech just produce more echolalia with their facilitators.

For reasons we don't understand, people who learn facilitated communication don't necessarily overcome antisocial behaviors. They may enjoy a respectful relationship with their facilitator, but fall back on primitive, even aggressive, communication with others. At this time, we can't predict whether success on the keyboard will let students overcome their various social and communication problems.

The effect facilitated communication has on a person's life will depend on many factors:

A) Can the facilitator fade support so that the student takes more control and may even learn to type independently?

B) Will the student develop competence with more than one facilitator, or will communication be limited to special times with that single facilitator?

C) Will the individual use facilitated communication to negotiate choices, or will he or she treat facilitated communication as a recreational outlet and continue using other behaviors for personal needs?

D) Will other people treat the individual with more respect, realizing that he or she understands and can report cases of mistreatment?

The invention of braille didn't cure blindness, nor did it make the world redefine blindness. It simply provided a valuable new technology. The same may be said of facilitated communication and autism. This technique is just one of many substitutes for verbal communication. Communication specialists have taught functional communication for years. Their results weren't always as dramatic as those of facilitated communication, but they still work with many students.

Do other communication aids work?

There are many alternatives to spoken or written communication. Chapter 11 ("What's a Communication Disorder?") reviews several systems people can substitute for speech or writing. Success depends on how well you match the language form or communication aid to the individual's ability.

For the time being, most parents want to try facilitated communication for a child with autism. This approach is new, the person who uses it can type anything in our vocabulary, and it takes no special training for another person to read the message. Facilitated communication offers the best replacement for verbal communication. However, it doesn't work for everyone, and it never works when the facilitator is absent unless the individual can master the keyboard alone.

The syndrome of autism embraces many neurological problems. Facilitated communication only concerns one, verbal apraxia. Problems with hearing, vision, and reasoning make other communication forms necessary. Ideally, every language system should have these features.

A) Wide recognition, understood by most people
B) Large vocabulary to express everything you want
C) Convenience, meaning that it doesn't require another person, certain locations, or special equipment

Common speech and writing combine the advantages of convenience, recognition, and vocabulary. Every other communication system sacrifices one or more of those qualities.

American Sign Language is the most versatile substitute for speaking or writing. A large population understands this language. Some communicate as quickly and accurately through sign language as others do with speech. However, not everyone can master this technique. People with neuromotor problems may find hand signs as hard to reproduce as speech. Learners who can't associate symbols or abstract gestures have trouble using more than a few basic signs.

Many people with autism use more than one communication form. For example, some use sign language, but have more skill with another gestural form of communication. Pointing to squares on a wall chart or on a picture board works well for some people. Others prove adept at flipping through laminated pictures attached to a key ring. Some can sort through a "vocabulary" of two or three hundred pictures faster than they can form clear hand signs.

When one communication form fails, it's helpful to have a backup system. If your child isn't near a picture board, or loses her key ring, she may need a few hand signs for emergency communication. A couple of picture cards in a wallet can help a good signer who is surrounded by people who don't understand her or his signing.

Technology keeps producing inventions such as voice synthesizers, talking picture boards, and other auxiliary communication devices. Before buying any of these products, you should ask: "Does this improve my child's expression?" "Will more people understand my child with this device?" "Will it offer my child a larger vocabulary?" "Is it more convenient, portable, or independent than other systems?"

Most of us use multiple communication systems—the telephone, letters, face-to-face conversations. Like us, people with autism need more than one way to communicate.

They won't all master the same systems. They need help to find which systems work best for them.

REVIEW

Facilitated communication is a technique that lets nonverbal people type with help from a facilitating partner. A few parents discovered this technique years ago, but professionals have just learned that many people may benefit from this approach.

Facilitated communication proves that some people with autism have no sensory or intellectual disabilities, only neuromotor problems (apraxia) that limit verbal communication. Some people who previously had been judged retarded can produce high–level communication with a facilitator's help.

Doug Biklen at Syracuse University and Rosemary Crossley at DEAL (Dignity through Education And Language), in Melbourne, Australia, have pioneered training programs for facilitators. Numerous other centers, including the Adriana Foundation and the National Autism and Communication Research Institute, offer training and information to facilitators.

Research needs to determine how many people with autism can actually benefit from this system. Skeptics claim that facilitated communication is just a "Ouiji board effect." So many people have tried this technique that there are probably indeed examples of wishful thinking, honest mistakes, or even deception. However, instead of using a bad example to discredit the system, we should find ways to validate messages from the keyboard. We haven't found a foolproof way to separate the language of the facilitator from the message of the "facilitated." Courts in Australia, however, have already accepted the testimony of a person using facilitated communication.

This technique proves that some people with autism are much more intelligent than formerly believed. However, the technique doesn't solve all of the other problems associated with autism, such as obsessive-compulsive disorders and other neurological challenges to freedom and independence.

Some people will have more opportunities for education or employment, thanks to facilitated communication. Others will still need help with daily life skills, especially when they don't have a keyboard handy.

All forms of language have limitations: they're not understood by enough people, the vocabulary is too small, or they rely on props or hardware. People often need a backup communication system, such as sign language or pictures, in case their primary system fails. We have to match individuals with the language forms that work best for them.

What else should I read?

Berger, Carol Lee J. "Unlocking the Literate Minds of Students with Autism Through Technology." For a copy, write: National Autism and Communication Research Institute, P.O. Box 25228, Eugene, OR 97402.

Biklen, Douglas. "Communication Unbound, Autism and Praxis." *Harvard Educational Review*, Vol. 60, No. 3 (August 1990).

Crossley, R., and McDonald, A. *Annie's Coming Out*. New York: Penguin, 1980.

Eastham, David. *Understanding: Fifty Memowriter Poems.* For a copy, write: Oliver-Pate, P.O. Box 4017, Station E, Ottawa, Ontario, K1S 5B1 ($5.50).

Eastham, Margaret. *Silent Words: A Biography.* (1992) Oliver-Pate, P.O. Box 4017, Station E, Ottawa, Ontario, K1S 5B1.

Remington-Gurney, Jane, Batt, Margaret, and Crossley, Rosemary. "Word Finding Problems." *Newsletter*, Dec. 1990, DEAL Communication Centre, 538 Dandenong Road, Caulfield 3162 Australia.

Schawlow, Arthur and Aurelia. "Our Son: The Endless Search for Help," in Brady, M.P., and Gunter, P.L., eds, *Integrating Moderately and Severely Handicapped Learners. Strategies That Work.* Springfield, IL: Charles C. Thomas, 1985.

13

What's the Best Approach to Education?

Make sure the school sees your child as an individual, not just as a label or disability. If the word *autism* becomes the focus, instead of the person, the student and his or her potential could be lost behind the label. Everyone involved in the educational plan needs to share a common view of the child in order to work toward the same goals. We can't expect the student to meet one set of expectations at home and another at school.

Education is the most important service for people with autism, but it can also be the most confusing. Federal law guarantees a free "appropriate" education for children. However, schools don't always know what's "appropriate" for children with this disability—and neither do many parents.

Parents often complain that school staff don't understand their child, and sometimes they're right. There's a shortage of teachers trained to deal with neurological disorders. A recent study by the U.S. government's Office of Special Education and Rehabilitation Services (OSERS) reports that 30 to 40 percent of teachers in special education don't have the training required for certification. Furthermore, approximately 25 percent of the staff in this field turn over every year.

Between the ages of five and twenty-one, a student may have sixteen years of special education. Most of those students will have a brand new teacher for four of those years, while for five or six years, the teacher won't have had the training required to be fully certified! In some communities, no one in the school district has even seen a student with autism until the first child enrolls. Perhaps that will be your child.

Parents expect the professionals to plan the child's education, maybe even overcome the disability. As nonprofessionals, the parents want to trust the "pros." But, the family may understand the learning disability better than the staff.

Ideally, teacher and parent will agree on what makes an education appropriate for a particular child. There are key questions that need to be addressed. What is the purpose of education for this child? How does this student learn? When the school and the family agree on these issues, the student has a better chance of succeeding.

What is the purpose of education?

The purpose of education doesn't change just because the child has a disability. To educate means "to rear, to elevate, to develop." We train the young because we want them to become competent adults. However, we sometimes overlook the goals of competence and independence because so many traditions have shaped our view of education.

"Education for all" doesn't mean universal preparation for college, nor does it mean six hours of activity, five days a week, until graduation. An appropriate education is supposed to prepare the student for his future, as a citizen and, hopefully, as a taxpayer. Some students with autism will need specialized training to master self-help skills, learn a nonvocal communication system, and practice necessary social behaviors.

Typical students don't learn their life skills at school, they learn them at home, watching and interacting with family members. Children ask thousands of questions from the time they begin to speak. They watch *Sesame Street* and listen to family discussions. Some have hobbies and part-time jobs. Meanwhile, the schools supplement the average student's general learning with academic skills, generally designed for the college–bound.

Unfortunately, many schools don't know what to teach children with severe learning disorders or social problems. Some districts offer little more than day-care for students considered learning disabled.

By age eighteen, most high school graduates are ready to earn a living or begin professional training. They know how to shop, get around the community, entertain themselves, make friends, and "get a life." Most of those skills weren't taught in school. Society taught them.

Unfortunately, children with autism have trouble learning by example. They don't pick up all of our social clues. The communication disorder makes it hard to learn from conversation and discussion. Sensory problems can distort sights and sounds. Neurological disorganization may interfere with reasoning ability.

These children need help to learn the things we consider obvious. They need to practice life skills, not just "reading, writing and 'rithmatic." Some, like Dustin Hoffman's character in *Rain Man*, learn school subjects very well, but can't apply the math and reading to a practical task like grocery shopping.

Dr. Anne Donnellan, author of several important books on autism and professor of education at the University of Wisconsin, suggests a simple principle for educational planning. She calls it the rule of "functionality." Donnellan recommends that teachers ask this question to decide if a particular learning task will be useful for the student:

> If a student can't complete a task, will someone else have to do it for him?

Tasks like pounding on pegboards, singing rhymes, or memorizing Shakespeare don't pass the test for functionality. No one *has* to do those things for the student. But dressing, shopping, and doing laundry all have to be done by someone. When students can do those things for themselves, they have become more functional.

Ideally, we want to help each student reach the goals of freedom and independence. When a student has a disability like autism, the school faces more accountability than with a typical student. The school takes responsibility for training the child in functional skills, tasks that are not part of the regular college preparation program. Some of these children will attend college, but they still need more functional training than the typical student.

Neither parents nor teachers should assume that the diagnosis of autism puts a ceiling on a child's potential. Some of these students will develop remarkable talents in music, art, and even academic areas. A growing number go on to college. A few, such as Temple Grandin, earn a Ph.D. However, we shouldn't confuse a high grade level or having a college degree with success. The happiest people with autism are those who learn personal independence.

How do students with autism learn?

Students with autism learn like the rest of us, by responding to and interacting with our environment. We seek experiences we enjoy and avoid those we don't. This principle governs most human behavior. Like other students, those with autism follow their own interests, not necessarily their parents' or teachers'.

Problems arise when the student doesn't experience the environment as others do. The environment might be the same, but neurological differences can change the experience for the individual. Music to one person's ears could be irritating noise to another. If beauty is in the eye of the beholder, pleasure, adventure, and discovery are in the mind of the beholder as well.

The environment offers a combination of tastes, smells, sights, sounds, and textures. Each person notices these a little differently. Someone with damaged or distorted senses gets a very different sensation. A reward for one person could be an ordeal for another.

Research shows that people with autism have many neurological irregularities. Some affect a single sense, while others make it hard for the person to connect information from several sensory systems. A student with autism may process sounds at a different rate than they notice sights. For such learners, life could seem like a movie with the sound track run at the wrong speed, forcing them to ignore one sense to concentrate on the other.

In *Autism and Life in the Community*, Dr. Marcia Datlow Smith explains,

Autism is associated with unconventional reactions to sensory stimulation. Apparent disregard for some types of stimulation might be observed; for example, someone might speak, and there could be no sign of acknowledgement, or there might be a strong reaction to certain stimuli, such as hypersensitivity to sound. The individual might have a fascination with certain types of stimulation including smells, visual events such as spinning objects, or sounds. Textures might also be highly appealing. An individual with autism might be fascinated by the feel of a piece of lint, and hours of enjoyment might be derived from watching a string twirl. Many of the repetitive behaviors associated with autism, such as rocking, finger flicking, and twirling, at least in part, serve the purpose of providing sensory stimulation.

Abnormal responses to stimulation explain many of the symptoms of autism. They can also offer clues to the individual's learning style. Smith explains, "Sensory patterns associated with autism can be used constructively in teaching situations by using the preferred stimuli as a reward for desirable behaviors. Identifying sensory interests, and using the preferred stimuli as reinforcers, is a valuable method of motivating individuals with autism."

When one of the senses offers a preferred route for stimulation, it's also an effective pathway to learning. Fortunately, most skills can be learned through more than one of these routes. Students with hearing problems may learn best by seeing, or vice versa. Touch can substitute for sight when the message is written in braille. Individuals with poor reasoning skills may be able to memorize enough information to get by.

Do students with autism have common learning disabilities?

As we saw in Chapter 4, there can be tremendous differences among these students. Intelligence tests have recorded I.Q. scores from below 10 to more than 150. About two thirds of the people with autism appear to have some degree of mental retardation. They also have other impairments that won't be reflected accurately by the standard tests of intelligence.

A test score doesn't identify the problems behind that score, such as language difficulties, short attention span, or a confused reaction to stimulation in the classroom. A child with good vision and memory could seem competent, even "gifted" according to a written test, while another has neuromotor problems that lower his score because he can't physically write the answers. Yet they may both need carefully structured social experiences and training in self-help skills. In other words, I.Q. test scores may reveal little about your child's intelligence or about his abilities or disabilities

191

because such tests are not designed for people with autism. At best, those tests are imprecise and unable to identify some of the extraordinary skills that sometimes accompany autism.

You must look at the students as individuals, not just as children with autism. Pay attention to their personal choices, what Dr. Smith calls "the preferred stimuli." Next, look at each child's performance in different developmental areas.

Most learners with autism have serious delays in communication and social behavior, no matter how well they test in school subjects. A single student may show different rates of progress in such wide-ranging areas as language understanding, language expression, social development, motor development, and self-help.

On the one hand, you must look at the individual's strengths and weaknesses. On the other hand, studies on autism teach us to expect some fairly common learning patterns. The University of North Carolina's Division TEACCH (Treatment and Education of Autistic and related Communication handicapped CHildren) publishes some of the most helpful information about teaching children and adults with autism.

Research at Division TEACCH shows that many people with autism have strong visual and spatial skills. Most have better rote memory than reasoning ability, or understanding of cause and effect. Teachers can use this information to design lesson plans for students. Some learners can't follow spoken instructions; they need to be shown.

The most important thing is for the teacher to understand how the student picks up signals. A picture chart or a calendar with a written schedule lets students use their understanding of space to overcome misunderstandings of time and sequence. The best teachers learn to work with the individual's strengths, the preferred stimulus. Otherwise, repetition is useless.

Why are there so many approaches to education?

The first chapters of this book explained how long it has taken for us to realize that neurological problems cause autism. Before we found this out, educators and psychologists experimented with a variety of learning theories and techniques. For reasons we can't always explain, many approaches seemed effective for a few, but not for all students.

Part of the mystery involves the differences between students. Almost any serious attempt at education will help some of the students some of the time. For this reason, many of the earliest theories of education still have believers. However, careful evaluation at Division TEACCH and other research centers is making a difference. Education is becoming more of a science and less of a guessing game.

Many professionals began their careers before we had information about the biological and neurological differences behind autism. Chances are, the staff in your child's school has little or no experience in autism. Teachers, psychologists, and therapists often turn to the library for information. Sometimes they read articles written during different eras and dealing with more than one type of autism. This confuses many teachers, as well as parents. Some get the impression that no one really knows what's best.

Your guide through these many theories of autism should be your child. Whenever you run into another idea, ask yourself if this approach really sounds like your child. Are the problems treated by this method the problems of your child? How would he or she react if you did this?

Good teachers know how to adjust theory to suit the individual student. Many borrow ideas from more than one source, including:

    A) Operant conditioning
    B) Gentle teaching
    C) Imitation therapy
    D) Daily Life Therapy

E) Physical therapy

F) Communication therapy

A) *Operant Conditioning* and the practice of behavior modification were highly praised in the 1960s when Dr. Ivar Lovaas at UCLA began his research. Dr. Lovaas took the position that no one could understand (or change) any biological cause behind the child's behavior. The behavior would change, however, if others provided rewards and punishments to force the learner's cooperation. One of the key terms used by Dr. Lovaas and his followers is *compliance training*. In other words, the child is first taught to comply with the teacher.

In the last twenty years Dr. Lovaas has changed many of his techniques. He doesn't use harsh punishments as in the past, and the approach has become more positive. However, the philosophy remains the same: The child must learn to behave as the teacher decides.

A common goal of these teachers is the removal, or extinction, of any abnormal or "autistic" behaviors. For example, the teacher may spend months working to get eye contact from the student. The teacher may use verbal cues, demanding, "Look at me!" If these prove useless, the teacher introduces rewards, such as candy, every time the student looks the teacher in the eye. If the student refuses, the teacher may shout the request again, or turn to a light punishment, spraying water in the student's face.

Followers of this technique generally focus on academic skills and training the student to hide or camouflage odd behaviors that others might notice. Some of Lovaas's students learn habits that make them look more like typical youngsters. The program works best with very young children who have near-normal speech and academic ability. He calls graduates of his preschool "apparently normal." But, *apparently* only means "appears like." As we know, there is no cure for autism.

Whether these students can go through adult life "appearing normal" is another question. The world these children grow into won't offer ongoing operant conditioning.

No one will be there to give them M&M's for good behavior or a reprimand for hand-flapping. Critics complain that operant conditioning doesn't have long-lasting effects because the teacher, not the student, sets the agenda. Once the teacher is gone, his or her influence starts to fade.

B) *Gentle teaching* offers the greatest contrast to operant conditioning. Dr. John McGee, one of the leaders of this movement, believes that even the most violent or withdrawn individuals can be reached through gentleness and affection. He notes that people with severe behavior problems have very little positive contact. Other people usually try to constrain them or force them into compliance, which makes them dread human contact. They need to learn that the company of others can be rewarding or pleasurable.

Before teaching any particular skill or behavior, the teacher must gain the student's confidence. There can be no punishment or negative contact, only acceptance. The student needs to experience pleasure and sharing with other people. Then, and only then, can the teacher begin to shape behaviors that will make the person easier to live with and more accepted by society.

Videotapes of Dr. McGee's work show that he has made dramatic progress with some severely disabled, even violent, individuals. People have called his work nothing less than miraculous. His writings explain how to apply the theory to a broader variety of students.

The practice of gentle teaching has influenced many teachers. But many wonder if other people can apply this as well as Dr. McGee and his few trained followers. Another big question is whether or not this theory applies to learners who already have pleasurable social experiences, or only the most severely disabled and isolated.

C) *Imitation therapy* was first developed by Barry and Suzanne Kaufman as a home treatment plan for their own son. When they couldn't find professional help that offered hope for their child at a very early age, they decided to experiment. The Kaufman's began with the belief that their child chose to withdraw into his own world and needed to be coaxed and encouraged to interact with them.

The Kaufmans gave their son twelve hours of play therapy each day. Instead of making the child follow their lead, they imitated his every behavior in the belief that the child needs to discover his power to interact with others. In general, the parent/therapist copies the child until the student shows interest in responding, taking turns, and accepting direction from the therapist.

Barry Kaufman explains this technique in the books *Son-Rise* and *A Miracle to Believe In*. He and his wife also operate the Options Institute, a training center for children with autism and their parents. Some families travel a great distance and pay expensive tuition to learn this approach from the Kaufmans.

Imitation therapy was originally criticized because the Kaufmans seemed to make unrealistic claims. However, some professionals now include imitation therapy in preschool programs. It seems that some of the techniques are helpful for certain children, though few people recommend twelve hours of daily therapy or taking a child out of school for home-based treatment.

D) Daily Life Therapy is the name Dr. Kiyo Kitahara gave to the unique educational program and the two residential schools she founded, one in Tokyo and one in Boston. Unfortunately, Kitahara never published data on her students or their progress. When other professionals asked her for an evaluation of her program, Kitahara would answer, "My students are my research." However, Dr. Kathleen Quill reviewed Daily Life Therapy for the *Journal of Autism and Developmental Disorders* shortly before Kitahara's death in 1989 (Vol. 19, No. 4).

Before the Boston school opened, many families in the United States sent a child with autism and the mother to Japan in order to enroll in the first Higashi (Daily Life Therapy) School. Dr. Kitahara's theories grew out of Asian philosophy related to the theory of ying and yang, two opposite but complementary forces of nature. She believed these forces need to be balanced and that children with autism have an imbalance that causes anxieties. This destroys their confidence and prevents them from learning or doing things on their own.

Most students at the Higashi School live in the dormitories. They spend no time alone, attending classes five and a half days a week. Every activity is done in groups. They brush their teeth together, have strenuous gym classes together, write in their notebooks together. The only private activity is the use of the toilet, a skill which every student appears to learn quite early in the program.

Videotapes produced by the Higashi School show children in orderly classrooms, group musical performances, and gymnastic activities. Well-trained staff members supervise the children. Whenever a student hesitates or appears out of step, a teacher quickly comes to the rescue.

Tuition is currently fifty-six thousand dollars a year. Obviously, few families can afford this, unless their school district will pay, as sometimes happens within Massachusetts. The program is internationally known, with students sometimes coming from distant states or countries. The school bases its success on these features: intensive control and routine, strenuous physical exercise, large staff numbers, and constant positive reinforcement of students. Some of these policies could be adopted by a local school district. The Kitahara program, however, is much more like a Japanese school than an American one.

Some children seem to make remarkable progress at these schools. The intensive daily schedule and round-the-clock staff keep most problem behaviors away. However, there are no studies that report what happens to the students after they leave the Higashi school. Do they maintain their behavior? After years without free time, can they manage on their own and make decisions? Or do they need constant supervision in order to function as they did at school?

E) *Physical therapy* and exercise offer benefits for many students. However, some people make unrealistic claims about intensive physical therapy. Many professionals in this field recommend moderation. They warn against "too much of a good thing." Chapter 9 explains the techniques of sensory integration, which appear to help many students.

Many of the bizarre and disabling behaviors associated with autism seem to grow out of the individual's unusual response to stimulation of one or more of the sensory systems. Occupational therapists and physical therapists use the term *sensory defensiveness* to describe negative or abnormal responses to common environmental stimuli. Antisocial behaviors such as avoiding touch, running away, or demanding "time out" can often mean the child finds our company disturbing. Our sounds, our unpredictable movements, and our odors can all upset a child with sensory defensiveness.

Sensory integration can play a valuable role as part of a comprehensive school program. Using strategies such as exercise, massage, and tactile play, some children can overcome sensory problems that interfere with learning and social interaction. An occupational therapist needs to design a program for the individual and train the teacher to use those activities as part of the daily school experience.

Many parents know their child seems calmer after certain activities. Occupational therapists can often explain this in terms of the individual's physical and neurological development. This knowledge helps the teacher choose therapeutic activities for a learner. In some cases, sensory integration should continue as part of a daily schedule. In other cases, a student might overcome the sensory challenge.

Temple Grandin, author of *Emergence: Labeled Autistic*, invented a "hug machine" for her personal use. This machine encases her body, and a hand-controlled lever lets her adjust the amount of pressure. The deep joint pressure she gets from the hug machine seems to calm her, as massage might. Some preschool children have learned to use this machine, and occupational therapists are evaluating its success.

F) Communication therapy is essential for any good education program. Adults and children with autism may need ongoing evaluation and recommendations from a therapist in this field. Chapter 11 discusses a variety of approaches used for different kinds of students.

Communication therapists used to work primarily on stuttering, lisping, and other problems of vocal language. A new specialty is called pragmatics, an approach that considers the interaction and context of communication, not merely the sounds of language. The emphasis has shifted away from spoken language to a wide variety of gestures and behaviors that a person may use for expression. Pragmatic communication therapy deals with the effectiveness of communication and how well it serves the learner's needs, not just how it sounds to the listener.

Therapy begins with an assessment to evaluate how the learner currently communicates. How much does he understand? Which is the best method of reaching him? Speech? Writing? Another way? What are the problems or limitations of expression? Which behaviors carry a meaning to the parents or the teacher?

The assessment should show you the best, the easiest, pathway to communicate with a particular student. A nonverbal and illiterate person can often learn successful expression through sign language or other gestures. Once you recognize the student's current skill level, you can set learning goals. The goals should challenge the learner to attain new levels of fluency, but they must be reachable. The student needs to experience success, not failure.

Therapists who apply the theory of pragmatics don't take the student out of class to practice one-on-one communication in a separate environment. They teach the parents and teachers to increase communication in the classroom and the home.

First, the student needs opportunities to communicate. Sometimes this means changing the environment so the child must communicate. If favorite toys and snacks are deliberately put out of reach, the student can't help himself. He has to communicate his wish to a taller person.

Make the student depend on communication. Then, teach a requesting behavior (pointing, signing, etc.). Finally, reward the student every time he or she uses the requesting behavior. Gradually, the learner comes to recognize the essentials of communication:

A) Sometimes we need other people's help to get what we want.
B) We must signal or speak to show others what we want.
C) It works better to use a signal others like (pointing, gestures, or speech) because they don't cooperate when I scream, cry, or throw things.

A person with autism may take years to learn these rules of communication. Like us, they need to practice behaviors that meet personal needs without annoying or repelling other people. They need to discover that cooperation works better than violence or tantrums. This communication training is often the most important part of a school program.

What's an appropriate education?

Together, parents and teachers need to arrive at a shared vision of the child and his or her potential. They have to see the same strengths and weaknesses in order to agree on educational goals and strategies. The family should help the school teach skills that will make the student as independent and socially adjusted as possible. Parents can reinforce these skills at home.

An appropriate education begins when all concerned look at the student's personal learning style and skills. Next, all the teachers (including those at home) need to agree which new skills would make the student more functional and independent at home and at school. They may be skills like crossing the street, reading signs in the community, or using a bank account.

Educational goals must have value for the student, not just for the teacher or parent. Experienced teachers know it's easier to teach a student what she *wants to learn*, rather than what the teacher might prefer to teach. If the child finds personal satisfaction in a lesson, she pays more attention, learns faster, and repeats the learned behavior more often.

Sometimes parents and teachers can't agree where to start on an education plan. The child may have many challenges to deal with. For example, a single student might have all of these problems:

A) "Autistic" behaviors (hand-flapping, rocking, or spinning) that interfere with school work and bother other students.

B) Serious social delays that keep the child from sharing toys or space with others. Perhaps the child tries to escape or hits others.

C) Uneven academic skills that might let a student read and spell without comprehension. Or perhaps the student can do math assignments by memory, but doesn't understand premath skills, such as quantity (more or less).

D) A communication disorder that makes it hard for the teacher or parent to tell how much the child really knows, or how he or she expresses wants and dislikes.

E) Sensory problems that can cause bizarre behaviors and fears. Perhaps the child screams or flees from certain sounds, movements, or odors.

F) Difficulties in reasoning that prevent the student from understanding cause and effect or the sequence of events. This makes the school day seem confusing and disordered. The student may have problems like losing track of time or becoming extremely impatient.

REVIEW

Some educators call autism the ultimate learning disability, not because the students can't learn, but because their teachers need to discover the individual's learning style. Each student with autism may have different responses to the sights, sounds, and events of the classroom. The teacher can take nothing for granted. Each student will need an evaluation of communication skills, social development, and sensory perception. No single test will give all the information the teachers and parents need.

Make sure the school sees your child as an individual, not just as a label or a disability. If the word *autism* becomes the focus instead of the person, the student and his or her potential may be lost behind a label. Everyone involved in the educational plan needs to share a common view of the child in order to work toward the same goals. We can't expect the student to meet one set of expectations at home, and another at school.

Students with autism won't all develop the same skills. Some will speak, while others will use sign language or point to a picture board. But each can learn a functional form of communication. Each can learn to express needs, choices, and dislikes. The luckiest individuals learn functional skills as well as regular school work.

What else should I read?

Donnellan, Anne. *Progress Without Punishment: Effective Approaches for Learners with Behavior Problems.* New York: Teachers College Press, 1988.

Lovaas, O. Ivar. *The Autistic Child: Language Development Through Behavior Modification.* New York: Irvington Publishers, 1977.

McGee, John. *Gentle Teaching: A Nonaversive Approach to Helping Persons with Mental Retardation.* New York: Human Sciences Press, 1987.

What's the Best Approach to Education?

————Beyond Gentle Teaching: A Nonaversive Approach to Helping Those in Need. New York: Plenum Press, 1991.

Quill, Kathleen, et al. "Daily Life Therapy: A Japanese Model for Educating Children with Autism." *Journal of Autism and Developmental Disorders*, Vol. 19, No. 4 (1989).

Smith, Marcia Datlow. *Autism and Life in the Community*. Baltimore: Paul H. Brooks, 1990.

Schopler, Eric. *Teaching Activities for Autistic Children*, Vol. 3 in the series Individualized Assessment Treatment for Autistic and Developmentally Disabled Children. Baltimore: University Park Press, 1983.

14

Does It Matter Where Your Child Goes to School?

Common sense tells us a child has a better chance of learning normal behaviors around normal people. Yet children with autism already have typical role models in their families and neighborhoods. What's missing? We have to look beyond common sense to teach those who don't learn automatically from example.

We usually don't have to choose our child's classroom. The typical child goes off to the neighborhood school where she finds a room full of students the same age. A few families select a religious school or private academy, but most accept whatever the public school system offers.

Choice usually isn't a concern for the average child until college. Then the student and parents begin to ask: "Where are the best teachers?" "Which school offers the best program for this student?" and "What difference does the staff-to-student ratio make?"

These questions are important to ask, not only before paying out college tuition, but during the years of public education as well. But we usually don't ask, because we expect the average five-year-old to thrive in most learning environments.

When the student has a learning disability, such as autism, quality becomes an issue with the first day of preschool. What's best for the child depends on the learner as well as the school. The teacher's preparation, the support services, and the student population all affect the educational experience.

Do students with autism need a special classroom, or is it better for them to learn among typical students?

This question often pits parents against school districts. Sometimes the family wants a special classroom for students with autism, and sometimes the professionals do. In most states you will find a mixture of parents and teachers on each side of this issue.

In 1991 the Autism Society of America reported two legal victories for families who fought their school district's classroom assignment. The *Advocate* (Vol. 23, No. 4) reported both cases on a single page, yet the decisions appear to contradict each other.

In Montana, a family won the right for their seven-year-old son to spend the full day with typical students in a regular education classroom. Meanwhile, a federal district court in Oregon ruled that a local school district had to reimburse a family for the cost of sending their child out of state to a private residential facility.

How can this be? One family demanded, and got, full integration for a child with autism, while another family forced their school district to pay for a totally segregated private school! How could two courts in 1991 interpret the same law (Public Law 101-476) to satisfy both of these families?

It would be tempting to reach for the explanation that autism affects students so differently that some can benefit from integrated education and others cannot. However, the issue is really more complicated. Besides promising an "appropriate education," the law specifies "in the least restrictive environment." This leaves the door open to debate about whether or not it ever serves a child's interests to segregate him in order to receive special training. A related issue is whether disruption of the regular classroom by a severely disabled student justifies the school district to offer a separate classroom or even a separate facility.

It's often argued that "basic living skills" can't be taught in a regular education classroom, that students who cannot dress themselves, use the toilet alone, or communicate fundamental needs belong in a separate classroom. Behaviors such as violence, tantrums, and self-abuse are difficult to manage in a regular classroom, even with a full-time aide.

You might assume that common sense will determine whether a child will fit into a regular classroom or will require separate services. However, legal battles show that common sense hasn't led to agreement on this explosive issue. A court case will never determine what's best for every student with autism since each child has different needs and talents.

Remember, the key to the "education for all" law is the Individual Education Plan. The needs of a particular student take precedence over the policies of the school district. The law puts the welfare of the student above the values and economics of adults.

Why are some schools or classrooms segregated?

Public education has a long history in this country. In 1647 the Massachusetts Bay Colony required that every community of fifty or more families provide free public schools. Yet, two hundred years later, it was still illegal to teach blacks to read in some states. In the 1970s, Congress passed legislation that guaranteed every child, regardless of disability, a free appropriate education.

Our nation supported public education for 324 years before providing for children with severe learning disabilities. Some school districts offered "special education" in segregated classrooms or separate programs. Most states offered one or more residential programs called deaf schools or blind schools. However, many states made no provision for those with mental retardation, autism, or other disabilities that kept students from learning in a typical classroom.

For centuries, children with severe learning problems had no legal right to education. They depended on the good will of school districts, private charities, or their parents in order to get any education at all. Education became a civil rights issue for people with disabilities, as it had been for other groups. Finally, when federal law responded, many states and local school districts were caught unprepared. They didn't have the experience or technology to teach some students.

Before "education for all," schools had a simple rule for screening students: Can this pupil learn in the typical classroom without slowing down the rest of the class or requiring too much of the teacher's time? Students who needed more attention couldn't attend regular classrooms. Families had to teach these youngsters at home or look for a "special" program. Some parents organized cooperatives in church basements to teach one another's children.

Universities helped organize special schools for the teaching and research value. Psychologists, psychiatrists, teachers, and therapists wanted to study these children, and grouping the students together made it more efficient for professionals. Grateful parents were delighted to find programs with professional staff.

Programs for students with autism first began in heavily populated areas near large universities. Families soon heard that separate programs had the most experienced staff, and sending these students to "special schools" became the pattern. In some states, that's still true.

When Congress passed the "education for all" bill, school districts faced a challenge: either admit all children to regular classrooms, begin special programs, or send the most difficult students to private schools. Tuition at segregated schools paid out of the public school district budget usually cost less than start-up expenses for a new program. Segregated schools flourished. Some parents still prefer them, believing that a private education may be the best for their child. In some cases, that may be true.

Massachusetts uses segregation as a yardstick for disabilities. The state assumes that severely disabled students need the most segregation. The state therefore reimburses schools not for results, but for separating students with disabilities. This policy rewards segregation and lowers funding whenever a school makes a program more integrated.

Thirty or forty years of separate education set the pattern. Students of education learned half-truths: children with autism need specially trained teachers; a program with specially trained staff can do more for these students than the average teacher. These beliefs support the traditional segregation of students with autism from the typical student body. However, we know that students with autism don't all share the same learning disabilities, or limited potential. We also know that skillful teachers can sometimes integrate a student with special problems into a more typical learning situation. Special services can follow the student. The student doesn't have to travel to the service.

Do some students need a residential school?

Before the Education For All Bill, many families sought residential programs for children with developmental disabilities. Doctors and social workers routinely recommended sending the child away for the sake of other family members. Many state facilities were called schools, because the name sounded better than *institutions* or *sanitariums*. But the people living in those "schools" could be as old as seventy or eighty.

Residential services cost much more than day schools. Private programs charge up to eight thousand dollars a month. Few families can afford this unless insurance covers part of the cost. Occasionally, a school district will pay the tuition, though it costs a fortune by the time the student turns twenty-one.

Courts rarely authorize residential school referrals. A family has to prove that the student needs more than a day program, that he needs consistent, round-the-clock training seven days a week. Less comprehensive schools serve the student thirty or fewer hours a week, expecting the family to provide most of the child's training and care.

Some students with autism have trouble adapting to different environments. The more disabled the student, the more confusing he may find change. A totally stable environment, with unchanging rules and standard staff behaviors, simplifies things for the student.

But the questions remain. Does any student need a residential program? Are people with severe learning disabilities so different that they can't live in our world? Do they need teaching methods we can't provide in our homes and our schools?

Opinions on these issues are sharply divided, especially in the context of larger social changes that affect the way we look at disabilities and people with differences. In the early seventies, attorneys challenged the way we treated people with disabilities such as mental retardation and autism. For centuries we had treated them as incompetents, children who would never outgrow their dependence on parents or guardians. They, in fact, had no legal rights until lawyers filed class action suits on their behalf, especially those in institutions. The legal profession recognized that all persons born and residing in this country had full citizenship. A disability doesn't abrogate an individual's rights as defined by the Constitution.

This new view set off a series of changes that affected people with autism and their families. One such change is "informed consent," a legal requirement in medical treatment which says that no one can perform surgery or administer drugs without consent from the individual or his court-appointed guardian. Facilities can't confine, bind, or seclude persons without guardian approval. Teaching techniques, especially those that involve punishment or restraint, receive closer review than ever before.

Large institutions are closing or "downsizing" all over the country. Bills in Congress propose shifting federal dollars away from segregated facilities and directing the money toward community-based programs. New Hampshire, for example, became the first state to close its last residential program for people with developmental disabilities.

These changes haven't pleased everyone. A number of parents and professionals resist this deinstitutionalization movement, arguing that society can't serve and protect the most disabled people in the community. On the other hand, programs such as CSAAC (Community Services for Autistic Adults and Children) in Rockville, Maryland, offer another way. CSAAC prepares people with extremely severe disabilities to succeed in ordinary neighborhoods and work settings. The success of such an effort, however, requires a great deal of planning and public support.

In 1988 the Office of Special Education and Rehabilitation Services funded a five-university project to study "Management of behavior disorders in individuals with developmental disabilities." Dr. Robert Horner, chief director for the project, explained its purpose: "Research is changing the way we measure the success of behavior therapy. It is no longer enough to merely reduce problem behaviors. We now seek to increase the individual's options for community involvement, participation, and social contacts. Accordingly, our research will focus on 'real life problems' in 'real life settings.' " (Advocate, Vol. 19, No. 4.)

Unquestionably, the pendulum has swung away from separate residential programs toward integrated community services. Most students with autism face a future in "real life settings" and therefore need an education that prepares them for those challenges.

Dr. Anne Donnellan recommends that we adopt the "hypothesis of the least restrictive environment." While designing a student's education, it's better to *assume* he or she will live and work in an integrated environment. Always plan around that assumption.

If the student can't succeed in the least restrictive environment, teachers and parents can lower their expectations with no harm done. This is less damaging than underestimating a child's potential. That could lead to fewer challenges, making the student less prepared for opportunities in the future. Simply stated, it's better to aim too high and fall short than to set a lower goal that becomes a ceiling on development.

How important is integration?

This is a dangerous question. Many people question your motives when you ask what they think of integration. You may as well ask, "How important is freedom, or justice, or equality?"

Our society has a commitment to these words. People don't want these values challenged, weighed, or evaluated. Once you acknowledge a common commitment, however, most people will discuss practice and policy with you. We need to examine the practical side of these issues.

Does daily total integration prepare children for free choice and equal opportunities as adults? Or do some children need separate learning experiences to prepare them for more integration later on? At which point in time do we measure integration—during the school years, at some later time, graduation, employment, retirement? Does a statistic—like the amount of time an individual spends with nondisabled people—indicate integration or quality of life?

These are hard questions to ask, and even harder to answer in the abstract. People may agree on the ideal, but attaining that ideal in a real world is never easy. In a perfect world, everyone would have a commitment to these values. Each teacher could nurture students of every level in the same classroom. Students would accept differences in their classmates without judgment, teasing, or favoritism. Slow learners would flourish because fast learners would help them. In fact, a totally ideal world would have no learning disabilities or inequalities to resolve!

Chapter 13 makes it clear that the American education system is not an ideal world! Statistics show a serious shortage of teachers with training and experience in learning disorders. Most school districts can't afford to employ enough qualified teachers to staff even a few segregated classrooms. Training every teacher to deal with autism would make integration easier, but it sounds like a distant, if not impossible, goal.

Families often find that their choices fall short of the ideal. Schools rarely offer appropriate educational services in an integrated setting. More often than not, the child with a disability receives all meaningful training in a closed classroom with a few other special education students. Contact or "mainstreaming" classrooms may be assigned for legal reasons, not to nurture the student's interests or abilities. In settings like this, most parents cling to an experienced teacher, no matter how segregated the class, rather than asking for a less restrictive environment.

Common sense suggests a child has a better chance of learning normal behaviors around normal people. Yet children with autism have typical role models in their homes and neighborhoods. The problems of autism don't just disappear with social contact. If it were that easy, these children would start out on the right foot. The schools wouldn't have to "fix them."

We understand the neurological basis of autism well enough to know that we should reject the outdated myths about emotional causes. However, most people with autism will have social difficulties all of their life. This is not because they are left out of human company, or somehow taught to fear it, but because neurological problems distort the way they see, hear, and experience life. They simply don't pick up the same signals that the rest of us do, even when we're sharing the same experience in the same place at the same time! What does this mean, in terms of integration?

Does it mean they can't, or shouldn't, mix with us? *Hardly*. Many people with autism adapt to our customs, though our behaviors may seem unnatural to them. Our social rules were developed by the general population for its own convenience and comfort, not for the ease of people with sensory distortions and learning disabilities.

Does it mean these people learn better if they spend more time with nondisabled people? Do they learn more if we increase the number of nondisabled people they see every day? Does sharing space with people guarantee interaction? *Not necessarily*. A mathematical formula can't "guesstimate" the time needed, nor the ratio of people required, to integrate an individual successfully.

The Association for Persons with Severe Handicaps (TASH) published an overview of the issues of integration entitled, *"How Much Time Should Students with Severe Intellectual Disabilities Spend in Regular Education Classrooms and Elsewhere?"* The authors, Lou Brown and colleagues from the University of Wisconsin, encourage the integration movement, for they want to see children with disabilities in regular classrooms for a civil and democratic reason.

"The future leaders, taxpayers, service providers, and parents of children with disabilities," they write, "are in those regular classrooms. They need direct experience with the kinds of children they will produce and the diversity of citizens with whom they will associate."

This opinion seems to hold up after research studies of earlier integration movements. When people are separated or concealed from one another, misconceptions and stereotypes continue. Break those barriers, and the stereotypes fall apart. In a political, as well as a spiritual, sense, inclusion has value.

The more individuals who join the whole, the stronger the whole becomes. We do run the risk, however, of placing too much burden on the most fragile members. Why make learners with severe disabilities stay in classes that don't interest them or offer even a modest chance for success? We must consider the needs of the individual.

We don't send children to school in order to learn "studenthood." They go to learn skills that will help them out of school (childhood) and after school (adulthood). Brown reminds us that not all school activities transfer beyond the four walls. "Many experiences available in regular education classrooms are important for nonschool and postschool functioning, but many are not."

He also explains what educators mean when they use the term *generalization* to describe a common learning problem of students with autism:

"The performance of a skill under conditions that are different from those under which it was acquired is called generalization. The more intellectually disabled a student, the less confidence one can have that what was acquired in one environment will be performed acceptably in another. In short, as regular education classrooms are rarely real-life environments, instructions must be provided elsewhere."

In plainer language, this means that some learners can apply classroom training in the supermarket, and others can't. If some students can't take information from the school into the real world, it's better to teach them in the real world, at least part of the day!

There are many approaches to integration besides assigning the student to a typical classroom full-time. A technique called reverse mainstreaming, makes use of student volunteers from regular classrooms. The volunteers spend time in the special education student's room. This provides integrated contact with more structure and security for the student with the disability.

Different approaches make some form of integration a reasonable goal for every student, no matter how severe the disability. Success means matching the strategy to the abilities and interests of the individual student, and always carefully monitoring the individual's responses. When students use "escape" behaviors—refusing to go to school, or acting out in order to be sent from the classroom—it means they don't like their school situation.

Pay attention to signals from your child. If he wants more time with regular students, he will let you know. If she wants more time by herself or needs the security of a more controlled classroom, she'll find a way to tell you.

REVIEW

Special education has a short history compared to regular education. Students with disabilities once had no legal right to education, so few teachers were trained to deal with severe learning disabilities. Parents tolerated segregation, including referral to private schools, because many school districts had nothing else to offer.

Separate schools and special education classes became the norm, even in the early 1970s. When the "education for all" bill passed, it promised an appropriate education "in the least restrictive environment." But twenty years later, many families and school districts can't agree where an individual student will learn best.

Sometimes parents and teachers decide a particular student needs a segregated program, perhaps a residential school or a closed classroom with a full-time aide. More often, the adults arrange opportunities for mixing with typical students during part of the school day. Choosing activities for integration and designing the daily schedule should be part of the Individual Education Plan annually negotiated between parents and their child's teacher. No formula seems to work for every individual and we must watch the student's reactions. Does he want more, or less, time in regular education classes?

Integration is supposed to bring people together, but we're a nation accustomed to diversity. Our education system has to serve students with different needs. We shouldn't pay unnecessary attention to those differences, or make them barriers to opportunity.

What else should I read?

Smith, Marcia Datlow. *Autism and Life in the Community*. Baltimore: Paul H. Brooks, 1990.

Brown, Lou, et al. "How Much Time Should Students with Severe Intellectual Disabilities Spend in Regular Education Classrooms and Elsewhere?" *Journal of the Association for Persons with Severe Handicaps*, Vol. 16, No. 1 (1991).

15

What Will the Future Bring?

> Don't assume that someone with autism stops learning at age eighteen, twenty-one, thirty, or even forty. Your development didn't end at that age, and neither will your child's. With encouragement and support systems, people with autism can continue to learn throughout their lives, just like everyone else.

When a child shows developmental problems, a parent's first impulse is usually to look for a cure. That search may last for months, years, or even decades, depending upon the family and the quality of information available. Eventually, most parents focus on the future, asking hard questions. What will our son be like when he's grown? Will our daughter be able to work? To live in her own apartment? Can she be happy?

Future predictions are notoriously unreliable, for we simply don't know when breakthroughs in technology may revolutionize medical treatment or education. At this writing, the jury is still out on the two most recent treatments, facilitated communication (Chapter 12) and auditory training (Chapter 10).

Economics and politics will affect the way society views people with disabilities. Before 1971, no law guaranteed a free education for children with disabilities. Many kids had no schooling, and their families often had no help. They had to take care of their children around the clock or look for professional help within an institution.

Though we can't predict either scientific or social progress, it's certain that parents of children with autism will help determine many of the policies shaping their childrens' lives. Parent organizations can be an effective lobbying force for education, employment, and other entitlements.

Policies for the next twenty years are being planned today. Every parent should consider joining the Autism Society or another advocacy group. As the educator Ralph Mager once said, "People who don't plan where they're going are bound to end up somewhere else." The "somewhere else" could mean a workplace or residence your child won't like.

At this time, many older people with autism live in mental hospitals, sanitariums, and other institutions. They live there because they were born too soon. No one offered them preschool experience, communication therapy, or an appropriate education. Most were never even diagnosed with autism, but were labeled retarded, psychotic, or various combinations of the two.

Regardless of the diagnosis on their medical chart, many people in the fifties and sixties had bad experiences with drugs, shock treatments, even lobotomies. Some misguided "treatments" damaged patients beyond the hope of recovery. In some cases, it's hard to sort the symptoms of autism from the effects of poor treatment. Thankfully, your child shouldn't have to face the hazards of outmoded treatments today.

Don't judge the past by today's standards, but expect more from the future. Don't settle for untrained teachers, or staff who haven't kept up with current research. No educational program should make your child uncomfortable or anxious. If you notice new discipline problems at school, or your child seems more rebellious at home, find out what's going on. Someone may be forcing your child to comply with behaviors that confuse him or upset his sensory input.

Avoid programs that isolate your child or damage her self-image because such restrictive environments may protect a student at the cost of personal growth. Social disabilities may grow worse if you deny opportunities for choice and expression. Chapter 13, on education, discusses the importance of including the student's interests in the Individual Education Plan scheduled at the beginning of each school year.

How can you plan for your child's life as an adult?

Statisticians warn that predictions are never reliable for individuals. We can safely predict that our understanding of autism will continue to improve and that there will be steady progress in teaching strategies. However, knowledge of the future performance of an individual student remains as elusive as our own future. After all, none of us expected to have a child with autism!

Developmental disabilities make an individual's progress even more unpredictable than the average person's. Autism won't be noticeable at birth, nor for many months. Even after diagnosis, these children won't follow the same developmental pattern. They won't reach the same milestones, nor necessarily follow the same sequence in development. Some will read before they speak, others will have late-blooming skills that amaze their parents.

Authorities use the term *autistic spectrum* to describe how much people with autism vary from one another. This variation can't be explained by neurological disorders alone. Our educational philosophy and the way we treat our children will also affect their adult performance. We might not be able to predict their response to a treatment, but these guidelines could help you prepare for the best, or worst:

A) Keep as many options open as possible. Dr. Anne Donnellan recommends assuming that your child will need to learn money management, housekeeping, and how to use transportation systems such as the community bus service, carpools, and pedestrian pathways and crosswalks. Assume your child will need those skills and ask for appropriate training in the Individual Education Plan. If Johnny or Suzy doesn't reach those goals, your expectations haven't done any harm. On the other hand, if you started with goals that were too low, it will be harder to raise them later on.

B) Don't assume that people with autism stop learning at age eighteen, twenty-one, thirty, or even forty. Your development didn't end at that age, and neither will your child's. With encouragement and support systems, people with autism can continue to learn throughout their lives, just like everyone else.

C) Remember, there's a difference between the primary and secondary symptoms of autism: Dr. Leo Kanner prepared the first list of "autistic" symptoms in 1943. He observed antisocial behavior, lack of personal attachments, and poor emotional responses. However, none of the people he saw in the forties had the benefit of early childhood training or communication therapy.

Lack of education and ineffective treatments took a terrible toll on Kanner's first group of patients. It was natural for them to seem withdrawn and antisocial. Today, we realize that some of the symptoms Kanner listed weren't necessarily due to autism. They were caused by our misunderstanding of the disability and the inadequate training available in the past.

Medical science has changed the way we view autism. Now education is changing the outcome for students. We no longer expect the children to be hopeless, violent, or uneducable. They can be happy. No one can predict an individual's progress in school, or at work, but happiness doesn't depend on achievement alone.

What rights does a person with autism have?

People with autism, or another developmental disability, have a wide array of rights recognized by the federal government. First, and most enduring, they have the same rights and responsibilities of any other citizen in the United States. This means they can vote, own property, sue and be sued!

It surprises many parents to learn that they lose legal authority for their child at his eighteenth birthday. After that date, the child is presumed competent and responsible in the eyes of the law, unless the parents arrange for legal guardianship. Without guardianship, no one can control the finances or authorize medical treatment for a person of legal age.

Advocacy organizations and attorneys point out that it's in the best interests of some people to have a guardian. Without a court-recognized guardian, many people can't get medical care, because the law requires that hospitals and doctors get a patient's signature on an "informed consent" form. If the patient can't sign, or appears unable to understand, they can't meet the legal definition of informed consent. Hospitals may refuse treatment rather than risk a lawsuit that challenges informed consent to forcibly treat an individual.

Guardianships vary from state to state. Most require some type of competency hearing in which the parents or friends of the individual explain the nature of a person's disability and any limitations on his or her reasoning and judgment. A family member can ask to be appointed guardian, or an unrelated person may volunteer for the responsibility.

The court can assign full or partial authority to the guardian. "Full guardianship" means the person with the disability has no legal authority whatsoever. All legal authority is transferred to the guardian, so the individual is not considered responsible for debts or contracts. Guardians don't have to support their wards, nor can they be sued for their ward's behavior. Guardians protect people with disabilities, and the law protects the guardians from financial liability.

A "partial guardianship" leaves the person free to make decisions about anything except the specifics mentioned in the guardianship papers. Many parents arrange partial guardianship that merely puts financial decisions and consent for medical treatment in their hands. They want to protect their daughter or son's right to life-style choices, marriage, and voting.

Guardianship may restrict some of the individual's common civil rights. But people with disabilities have some special entitlements, including:

A) Special education
B) Supplemental Security Income (SSI)
C) Protection against discrimination as outlined by affirmative action Policies, the 504 regulations of the Vocational Rehabilitation Act, and the Americans with Disabilities Act.

Every school district in the country has to offer parents information regarding their rights and responsibilities under Public Law 101-476, the revised "education for all" bill. The school's literature should explain eligibility, evaluation, services, and appeal processes.

Children with disabilities or learning problems are entitled to special education between the ages of three and twenty-one. The state of Michigan offers special education up to the age of twenty-six, giving students more time to prepare for a job and to make the transition away from the family home. Many states offer preschool services to children from birth until the age of three.

It's important to make the most of special education, not just as a day program during childhood, but as a time to prepare a child for adult life. Educational services are paid for and guaranteed, but no such entitlements exist for adults. Some adults receive educational assistance from the Division of Vocational Rehabilitation, but benefits are based on individual case decisions. Your child may have trouble getting them.

SSI (Supplemental Security Income) is administered by the offices of the Social Security Administration. The program was designed for low-income people who are either blind, disabled, or elderly (age sixty-two or older). Benefits include a small monthly income (based upon need) and Medicaid coupons.

Before the age of eighteen, a child's eligibility for SSI is based on family size and income. Children from average-income families usually cannot qualify for SSI before their eighteenth birthday. After that date, the family income is no longer part of the eligibility formula. Adults with autism usually qualify for SSI and Medicaid coupons, unless they earn too much money.

Finally, the Americans with Disabilities Act makes it illegal to discriminate against people on the basis of a disability, or to allow barriers to their participation in community life, education, employment, transportation, or recreation. The details of this, and earlier legislation, are available through public agencies dealing with vocational rehabilitation, health and human services, and equal opportunities.

Every state has a private, nonprofit agency assigned by the governor to protect the rights of people with developmental disabilities. Called Protection and Advocacy Systems, these agencies can provide information about local resources and where to go with problems or complaints.

What can we expect from research in the future?

Parents sometimes complain that medical science hasn't helped them or their child. It's true that doctors aren't curing anyone of autism, but lack of a cure doesn't necessarily mean lack of progress. In less than fifty years, physicians have recognized and described autism for the first time in human history, moved beyond a psychogenic theory that blamed parents for the child's problems, and used autopsies and scanning technology to identify the neurological causes of autism.

In the meantime, professionals tried everything from psychotherapy to surgery. Many treatments were discontinued because of failure or bad side effects. In spite of a bad start, our medical understanding of autism has made substantial progress. We haven't had a breakthrough in surgery or medicine, but we've learned more about the sensory problems and learning patterns.

Research is on the threshold of answering some of our most pressing questions: What's the role of genetics? Can we identify autism through blood tests? and Which parts of the brain perform functions involved in autism?

Genetic studies of autism are making progress. In the 1980s Edward Ritvo pioneered this field (see Chapter 3: "What Causes Autism?"). Now many researchers are studying family trees, searching for genetic patterns. At the New England Medical Center, doctors are looking for microscopic evidence in blood samples.

Genetic research could soon help in the prevention and treatment of autism. If we find that some people have genetic characteristics that contribute to autism, we might offer genetic counseling. The same information might explain how much autism is tied to genetics, or perhaps related to other factors, such as prenatal illness. That might lead to vaccination or other protections for pregnant mothers.

Maybe we'll find a "biological marker" for autism, a blood test that will one day make diagnosis easier and more reliable. If that happens, we'll be able to recognize children with the biological characteristics even before they show symptoms of autism. The sooner we reach kids like that, the more we can do for them.

Biological markers might even reveal subtypes we haven't recognized before. Up to now, we've had to make the diagnosis based on the appearance or behavior of the child. Blood tests that identify subtypes might help us to match treatments to individuals.

Neuroanatomy is making exciting discoveries about the human brain. Recent technology—including magnetic resonance imaging (MRIs), positive emission tomography (PET scans), and electroencephalograms (EEGs)—lets researchers examine the brains of living subjects, while they are involved in problem solving.

Dr. Judith Rumsey recently completed a study of people who have autism combined with unusual memory skills. She directed this study at NIH headquarters in Bethesda. Magnetic resonance imaging provided a profile of every subject's brain. Then, PET scans provided images of blood flow as subjects solved problems or answered questions based on memory skill.

Finally, information from both MRI and PET scans were integrated into the same computer program. This technology simulates a three-dimensional model of the brain. Researchers can then "watch" a living person's brain at work, showing precisely which areas of the brain operate during certain thought processes or motor functions. It's as though scientists have finally found the first chapters of an owner's manual for the human brain.

Information from neuroanatomy will help occupational therapists and communication therapists recognize the challenges of students. Therapists will understand people with autism better than before, and they will know more about the typical brain as well.

Hopefully, educators can keep pace with biological research. At this time, too many educational theories compete for teachers' attention and parents' loyalty. When a parent and a teacher disagree during an Individual Education Plan session, no one really wins. Only the student loses. We need more long-term studies that show how students fare over a period of time under different school programs.

Researchers need to look for students who began school with similar skills and behaviors, but had different educational experiences. Careful matching of subjects should make it possible to evaluate the effects of different programs on student performance and life skills.

Professionals may not find a cure for autism, but they can improve habilitation. We need to make the most of available therapies, to abandon those that are useless, and promote those with proven value. Then, parents will find it easier to raise a child with autism. The rewards will be greater for all of us.

16

Where Can Parents Get More Information?

Often, the *Advocate* will publish information about treatments or research months before the news appears in professional journals.

There are many opportunities to read about autism. *Reader's Digest* and other magazines often carry human interest stories, especially those that offer happy endings. Hollywood hasn't ignored this disability either. *Rain Man* may be the only film applauded by the Autism Society; lesser films such as *The Boy Who Could Fly* use the disability to symbolize alienation and mystery.

Somewhere between the dry stacks of a medical library and the slick pages of a tabloid, you'll find useful information for parents. The following lists are not complete, because information, like water, takes many different directions—and it keeps moving! However, a person who wants to find out about autism, *as we understand it today*, should join an organization that will inform him of changes as they occur.

ORGANIZATIONS

Autism National Committee: 635 Ardmore Avenue, Ardmore, PA 19003 (215) 649-9139. Founded in 1990, this organization exists to provide an information network for people advocating better treatment and rights for people with Autism. There are no local or state chapters, only a national newsletter and annual conference. Membership is $20.00 a year.

Autism Society of America: 7910 Woodmont Ave., Suite 650, Bethesda, MD 20814 (800) 328-8476. Founded in 1965, a year after its sister organization in England, ASA has several thousand members, including chapters in every state. The society publishes a quarterly magazine (the *Advocate*), holds an annual four-day conference, and helps develop local chapters that provide information and referral. Dues range from $12.50 a year for students to $35.00 for families.

Autism Society of Canada: 2-20 College Street, Toronto, Ontario, Canada M5G 1K2. Like the ASA, the Canadian society publishes a newsletter and helps its local and provincial chapters provide information and services to members. In 1993 the Canadian and American Societies will sponsor their first joint conference in Toronto.

The National Autistic Society: 276 Willesden Lane, London, England, NW2 5RB. Founded in 1964, this was the first society to serve people with autism and their families. The National Society publishes the *Communicator*, and offers information and referral across the United Kingdom.

BOOKS BY PARENTS

Bratt, Berneen. *No Time for Jello: One Family's Experiences with the Doman-Delacato Patterning Program.* Cambridge, MA: Brookline Books, 1989. The mother of a son with cerebral palsy, Mrs. Bratt had frustrating experiences similar to parents of children with autism. She provides a documented history of her experience with the Doman-Delacato Patterning Program and identifies the professional organizations that censure the program that left her family "no time for Jello."

Callahan, Mary. *Fighting for Tony*. New York: Simon & Schuster, 1987. This book recounts problems raising a son with uncontrollable temper tantrums and learning disabilities. A former pulmonary nurse, Callahan turned to allergy treatments in search of a cure. She claims that her son's symptoms all disappeared after she eliminated cow's milk from his diet. She believes her son never had autism, but that cerebral allergies caused symptoms that looked like autism.

Christopher, Barbara and William. *Mixed Blessings*. Nashville, TN: Abingdon Press, 1989. The Christophers describe their experience trying to help an adopted son disabled by autism. They spared no effort or money in their search for help. Yet they encountered poor advice and bad treatments, including the Doman-Delacato Patterning Program (described more critically by Bratt).

Eastham, Margaret. *Silent Words: A Biography* (1992). Oliver-Pate, P.O. Box 4017, Station E, Ottawa, Ontario, K1S 5B1. Mrs. Eastham wrote this as a tribute to her deceased son, David. David's life and accomplishments make an inspiring story, but this book is even more fascinating because his mother explains how she taught this son with autism to read and uncovered a remarkable literary talent as a result.

Greenfield, Josh. *A Child Called Noah*. New York: Holt, Rinehart & Winston, 1971. This is the first of three books Greenfield wrote about his son, Noah. It covers the child's development, from diagnosis of autism through the search for appropriate early intervention. The author's experience with Lovaas in the late sixties shows that program once used aversives and punishments that would be unacceptable today.

Hart, Charles. *Without Reason: A Family Copes with Two Generations of Autism*. New York: Harper & Row, 1989. The author describes his experiences, first as a brother, then as a father, of a person with autism. Spanning the years from 1920 to 1989, the book shows the dramatic progress of research and services for people with autism.

Kaufman, Barry Neil. *A Miracle To Believe In.* Garden City, NY: Doubleday & Co., 1981. Following the better known *Son-Rise*, this book expands on Kaufman's "options theory" in which he claims "miracles will happen to people who believe in them." Many authorities on autism object to Kaufman's claims, yet some of the techniques he recommends in imitation therapy have found their way into professionally staffed preschools.

Kaufman, Barry Neil. *Son-Rise.* New York: Harper & Row, 1976. This may be the best known and most controversial book a parent has written on autism. The Kaufmans diagnosed their son at an unusually early age (17 months). They developed their treatment, which was later called imitation therapy. Reacting against the strong authoritarian model of the early Lovaas school, the Kaufmans decided to let their son take the lead in activities while they imitated him. Although there will never be empirical evidence to support the author's claims, this book received wide attention and even became a made-for-television movie with the same title.

Maurice, Catherine. *Let Me Hear Your Voice.* New York: Knopf, 1993.The author wrote under a pseudonym to protect her two young children, whom she considers "recovered" from their autism. At the time the book was written, her daughter was six years old and the son was only four. The mother has good documentation for the children's early diagnoses, but her expectation for full habilitation or "recovery" must be considered premature. The author attributes her children's success to Ivar Lovaas and his home-study program and urges other families to pursue early diagnoses and intervention.

Park, Clara Claiborn. *The Siege*. New York: Harcourt, Brace, World, 1967. The first and possibly most beautifully written book by a parent, *The Siege* covers the first eight years of Clara Park's daughter's development. Professionals consider this book a classic on the subject of autism. A later edition, printed in 1982, contains a forty-page epilogue covering a time span of fifteen years.

Stehli, Annabel. *Sound of a Miracle*. Garden City, NY: Doubleday, 1991. This book made people around the globe aware of a previously overlooked form of therapy that attempts to desensitize individuals to sound-frequency irritation. The author claims that twenty half-hour treatments made a miraculous difference in her daughter's behavior and learning ability. Many parents are pursuing the same treatment for their children, and researchers are currently looking into this subject.

BOOKS BY PEOPLE WITH AUTISM

Barron, Sean and Judy. *There's a Boy in Here*. New York: Simon & Schuster, 1992. This book, written by a young man with his mother's help, presents a somewhat confusing view of autism. It's difficult to be sure how much Barron can really remember about his childhood obsessions and how much he relies on his mother's memories. Together, they claim that he has "recovered" from autism due to the mother's persistence and refusal to let him withdraw. Barron may still have sensory and neurological problems that fit the definition of autism, but the author chooses to believe he has "recovered."

Grandin, Temple. *Emergence: Labeled Autistic* (1986). Arena Press, 20 Commercial Boulevard, Novato, CA 94949-6191. Dr. Grandin has a remarkable life story to tell. Although she has earned a Ph.D. in animal husbandry, teaches at Colorado State, and operates her own livestock consulting business, Temple readily calls herself autistic. She views autism as a collection of neurological problems and considers occupational therapy (vestibular, proprioceptive, and tactile stimulations) necessary for maintaining equilibrium. Her insights into her own feelings and behavior are useful for understanding less talented people with autism.

Miedzianik, David C. *I Hope Some Lass Will Want Me, After Reading All This* (1986). Child Development Research Unit, Nottingham University, Nottingham, England NG7-2RD (5 pounds sterling). Mr. Miedzianik's autobiography gives us insight into the mind of a more typical person with autism. His disability is quite apparent in his writing style. He is remarkably uninhibited and honest describing his experiences and limitations, but seems unable to draw conclusions or deal with complex issues.

Williams, Donna. *Nobody Nowhere*. New York: Times Books/Random House, 1992. Ms. Williams' autobiography reads like poetry, but her imaginative style raises questions about the author's reliability and her control of images and associations. She reports a history of childhood abuse and later sexual exploitation, making it difficult for the reader to sort out the effects of autism and the consequences of abuse. Her disturbing childhood memories seem to be influenced by a form of multiple personality disorder (MPD), rather than by autism alone.

BOOKS TO HELP EXPLAIN AUTISM TO CHILDREN

Amenta, Charles, M.D. *Russell Is Extra Special*. A Magination Press, Brunner/Mazel Publishers, 19 Union Square, New York, NY 10003 ($6.95). This twenty-page book is illustrated with photographs and is designed to help young readers understand the problems of autism.

Dalrymple, Nancy, Ph.D. *Learning Together*, Indiana Resource Center for Autism (IRCA) 2853 E. 10th St., Bloomington, IN 47405 ($2.00 plus postage & handling), Spanish & Korean versions available: This twenty-seven–page book is illustrated with drawings and helps children understand the behavior of other students in the school who have autism.

Gold, Phyllis-Terri, Ph.D. *Please Don't Say Hello.* New York: Human Sciences Press/Plenum Publications, 1986. (1-800-221-9369). The author is the mother of a young man with autism. She was also one of the founding officers of the Autism Society of America. This forty-six–page book has photo-illustrations. Originally published in 1975, this is one of the first books about autism written especially for children.

NEWSLETTERS

The *Advocate:* Quarterly Newsletter of the Autism Society of America, 7910 Woodmont Avenue, Suite 650, Bethesda, MD 20814 (1-800-3-AUTISM). Subscription by membership only ($20.00 a year, individual membership). This publication contains a mixture of articles contributed by parents and professionals. Often, the *Advocate* will publish information about treatments or research months before the news appears in professional journals.

Autism Research Review International: Quarterly publication of Autism Research International (formerly Institute for Child Behavior Research), 4182 Adams Avenue, San Diego, CA 92116 ($16.00 a year). Bernard Rimland, a psychologist and father of a son with autism, edits and publishes this review. Dr. Rimland is often associated with megavitamin treatments and orthomolecular psychiatry, but he also reviews other research trends in his quarterly.

Focus on Autistic Behavior: Published bimonthly by PRO-ED, Inc., 8700 Shoal Creek, Austin, TX 78758. This publication offers reliable, up-to-date information on autism from a variety of professional fields. Information is interesting, accurate, and "user friendly."

The *MAAP*: This newsletter features articles by and about "More Able People with Autism." Susan J. Moreno, Editor, P.O. Box 524, Crown Point, IN 46307 ($8.00 yearly). The *MAAP* focuses on issues concerning higher-functioning people with autism and their families. No other publication offers as much for this specialized population.

Sensory Integration Quarterly: Published by Sensory Integration International, 1402 Cravens Avenue, Torrance, CA 90501-2701 ($20.00 a year). Although written by and for professional therapists, this newsletter can easily be read and understood by nonprofessionals. The information is always reliable, and generally applicable to people with autism.

The Sound Connection: A Quarterly Publication of the Society for Auditory Integration Training: 19210 SW Martinazzi Avenue, Suite 110, Tualatin, OR 97063: free to members of Society

FOUNDATIONS

Adriana Foundation: 2001 Beacon Street, Room 214, Brookline, MA 02146. Kristi Jorde, mother of Adriana, began this foundation to encourage research on autism. However, the foundation now focuses on facilitated communication. It sponsors conferences, demonstrations, and workshops in most regions of the country.

Georgiana Organization: P.O. Box 2607, Westport, CT 06880. Founded by Annabel Stehli (author of *Sound of a Miracle*) and named for her daughter, this foundation promotes the practice of auditory training and sponsors training sessions for audiologists and therapists.

Where Can Parents Get More Information?

MISCELLANEOUS

Autism Society of America: Greater Philadelphia Chapter:
P.O. Box 156, Swarthmore, PA 19081. Members have produced a helpful annotated bibliography of recommended readings on autism. For a copy of the bibliography, or a catalog of the chapter's reprints and publications, write or call (215) 975-0125.

Autism Society of North Carolina: 3300 Women's Club Drive, Raleigh, NC 27612-4811. This state chapter of the Autism Society of America operates an extensive mail order service for books on autism. Write for an order form.

CSAAC (Community Services for People with Autism): 751 Twinbrook Parkway, Rockville, MD 20851. Founded by a mother who wanted community services for her son, CSAAC had earned a reputation for successful integrated employment and residential programs. Dr. Marcia Datlow Smith, the group's consulting psychologist, has authored many articles and handbooks on managing aggressive behaviors and developing successful job sites. Write for a free catalog of publications, or call (301) 762-1650.

Boston Higashi School: 2618 Massachusetts Avenue, Lexington, MA 02173. The Boston Higashi School, founded by Dr. Kiyo Kitahara, closely resembles the school she founded earlier near Tokyo. Most students reside at the school. Write for information about programs, philosophy, and costs.

Division TEACCH (Treatment and Education of Autistic and related Communication handicapped Children): 310 Medical School Wing E 222H, University of North Carolina, Chapel Hill, NC 27514. Division TEACCH is the oldest, and probably most respected, research center in the world specializing in autism. Division staff edit the *Journal of Autism and Developmental Disorders*, host teacher training sessions during the summer, and provide consulting services to school districts throughout the world.

Indiana Resource Center for Autism: Institute for the Study of Developmental Disabilities (ISDD) Library, 2853 East 10th Street, Bloomington, IN 47405. The Indiana Resource Center has produced several practical guides to education, lesson planning, social skills, and behavior management. Since their publications were funded by research grants, the center charges only a small fee for reproducing materials. For a free catalog write or call (812) 855-6508.

Michigan Society for Autistic Citizens: 530 West Ionia Street, Suite C, Lansing, MI 48933. This society operates a mail order bookstore, carrying over fifty titles on topics such as behavior management, education, families, subtypes of autism, and employment. Write for a free, annotated catalog, or call (517) 487-9260.

Grandin, Temple. *Thinking In Pictures.* New York: Doubleday, 1995. Oliver Sachs provides an introduction to this book, explaining his experiences with the author whom he has called "The Anthropologist from Mars." Dr. Grandin explains how she has used her extraordinary powers of visualization to learn and respond through image rather than language. This book is a fascinating update to her earlier work and is vastly superior in style.

Index

Index

Index

Index